ひろがりが欲しかった。明日をつくる部屋だから。

ひとつの部屋に何種類もの家具を置くと、それだけでとても狭く見えてしまう。色、素材、カタチ、高さなど、ひとつの基準をきめて揃えてみると、ほら、こんなにすっきりした部屋が生まれてくるのですね。ヤマハシステムファニチャー。基本となるボックスをタテに、ヨコに、自由に組み合わせて、収納ダンスや飾り棚をつくりあげるクオリティの高いシステム家具。和服をきれいにしまう桐盆つきのものや、ロングドレスをかけるタテ長の収納室など、バリエーションも豊富です。もちろん、あとから少しづつボックスを追加して収納力を高めてゆくことも可能。ぎゃくに、最初は必要最少限の組み合わせからスタート、という方法もとれるわけですね。表面仕上げは木目4種。まずはインテリアのトーンをきめて、それから計画的に家具や小物をふやしてゆく。何気ない1枚の絵も、こんな部屋なら輝いて見えるはずです。

SYSTEM FURNITURE D-SERIES

これからはシステム家具・システムキッチン

キッチンが新しいライフスタイルを教えてくれる。

キッチン文化の時代だと言われます。いま、キッチンは生活をエンジョイするための新しい舞台として美しく生まれ変わりました。お客さまとの語らいを楽しむのも、キッチンルーム。呼んだり、呼ばれたり。人とのお付き合いがもっと楽しく、充実したものになるでしょう。システムキッチンを考えることは、新しいライフスタイルを考えることにもなります。写真のプランは、DK-1シリーズ アボカドグリーンを使ったファミリーキッチン。気軽でモダンなキッチンです。ヤマハユーティリティは8月発売予定になります。

MODERN BRAZILIAN ARCHITECTURE

現代ブラジル建築

: Architecture

1980年8月1日発行　第17号

発行者＝室谷文治
監修＝上田篤
担当編集者＝ウンベルト八巻
プロダクション・エディター＝栄 美智子

表紙デザイン＝丸茂喬司

アドヴァイザー＝
ナディル・アルダン（テヘラン）
ジョナサン・バーネット（ニューヨーク）
クレイグ・エルウッド（ロサンゼルス）
R・バックミンスター・フラー（フィラデルフィア）
ビル・N・レイシイ（ニューヨーク）
ディヴィッド・ルイス（ピッツバーグ）
槇文彦（東京）
イサム・ノグチ（ニューヨーク）
シーザー・ペリ（ニューヘヴン）
バーナード・ルドフスキー（マラガ）
ピーター・スミスソン（ロンドン）

印刷・製本＝
共同印刷株式会社
取次店＝
東販　日販　大阪屋　栗田出版販売　誠光堂

ロゴタイプ・デザイン＝脇田愛二郎

発行所＝
株式会社 プロセス アーキテクチュア
東京都文京区小石川3-1-3
電話　東京（03）816-1695・1696
振替　東京6-57446　郵便番号112

定価＝2,900円　送料＝250円

翻訳＝山本圭介

禁無断転載

IMPRESSIVE SCENE OF BRASILIA
by Atsushi Ueda
ブラジリアの印象　上田篤　　5

O. ニーマイヤーのスケッチから
SKETCHES BY OSCAR NIEMEYER　　14

NOTES ON THE MODERN BRAZILIAN ARCHITECTURE
by Carlos A. C. Lemos
現代ブラジル建築概観
カルロス・A・C・レーモス　　8

BRAZIL—KALEIDOSCOPE OF ARCHITECTURE
by K. Narumi + H. Yamaki
ブラジル——建築のカレイドスコープ
鳴海邦碩＋ウンベルト八巻　　148

CARVALHAL RESIDENCE　　Architect : Decio Tozzi
カルバリアウ邸　設計：デーシオ・トッズィ　　20

ABREU RESIDENCE　　Architect : Decio Tozzi
アブレウ邸　設計：デーシオ・トッズィ　　24

ITORORÓ VILLAGE URBAN RENOVATION　Architect : Decio Tozzi
イトロロー再開発　設計：デーシオ・トッズィ　　26

CAMPOS DO JORDÃO TELEPHONE EXCHANGE　Architect : Ruy Ohtake
カンポス・ド・ジョルドン電話交換局　設計：ルイ・オータケ　　30

IBIÚNA TELEPHONE EXCHANGE　Architect : Ruy Ohtake
イビウーナ電話交換局　設計：ルイ・オータケ　　32

BANESPA BUTANTÃ BANK　Architect : Ruy Ohtake
バネスパ・ブタンタン銀行　設計：ルイ・オータケ　　34

CETESB LABORATORY　Architect : Ruy Ohtake
セテスビ研究所　設計：ルイ・オータケ　　36

ÁGUAS DA PRATA BALNEARY　Architect : João Walter Toscano
アーグアス・ダ・プラタ保養所　設計：ジョアオ・ヴァウテル・トスカーノ　　38

ARARAQUARA UNIVERSITY CAMPUS　Architect : João Walter Toscano
アララクァーラ大学　設計：ジョアオ・ヴァウテル・トスカーノ　　44

JULIO DE MESQUITA FILHO HOSPITAL　Architects : F. Penteado & T. Tamaki
ジューリオ・デ・メスキータ・フィリオ病院　設計：F・ペンテアド＆T・タマキ　　48

CALUX KINDERGARTEN　Architect : Paulo Mendes da Rocha
カルックス幼稚園　設計：パウロ・メンデス・ダ・ローシャ　　52

CECAP TAUBATÉ HOUSING DEVELOPMENT　Architects : Bonilha & Sancovski
セカッピ・タウバテー・ハウジング　設計：ボニーリャ＆サンコーヴィスキー　　54

MORUMBI OFFICE BUILDING　Architects : Bonilha & Sancovski
モルンビー・オフィス・ビルディング　設計：ボニーリャ＆サンコーヴィスキー　　58

J. O. MAIA RESIDENCE　Architects : Bonilha & Sancovski
J・O・マイア邸　設計：ボニーリャ＆サンコーヴィスキー　　60

VERONEZZI RESIDENCE　Architects : Bonilha & Sancovski
ベロネッズィ邸　設計：ボニーリャ＆サンコーヴィスキー　　62

PIRAQUÊ INDUSTRY　Architect : Marcello Fragelli
ピラケー・インダストリー　設計：マルセーロ・フラジェリ　　64

2

PONTE PEQUENA METRO STATION　Architect : Marcello Fragelli　67
ポンテ・ペケーナ地下鉄駅　設計：マルセーロ・フラジェリ

L. GUEDES RESIDENCE　Architect : Joaquim Guedes　71
L. ゲーデス邸　設計：ジョアキン・ゲーデス

MOREAU RESIDENCE　Architect : Joaquim Guedes　73
モレアウ邸　設計：ジョアキン・ゲーデス

BEER RESIDENCE　Architect : Joaquim Guedes　76
ビーエル邸　設計：ジョアキン・ゲーデス

CARAIBA NEW TOWN　Architect : Joaquim Guedes　78
カライーバ・ニュータウン　設計：ジョアキン・ゲーデス

IBM EDUCATIONAL CENTER　Architects : Pontual Associados　82
IBM教育センター　設計：ポントゥアール・アソシアドス

COSAMA RESERVOIR　Architect : Severiano M. Porto　84
コザーマ貯水槽　設計：セベリアーノ・マリオ・ポルト

SHUSTER RESIDENCE　Architect : Severiano M. Porto　86
シューステル邸　設計：セベリアーノ・マリオ・ポルト

PORTO RESIDENCE　Architect : Severiano M. Porto　90
ポルト邸　設計：セベリアーノ・マリオ・ポルト

ZANETTINI RESIDENCE　Architect : Siebert Zanettini　94
ザネチーニ邸　設計：シーギベルチ・ザネチーニ

BANESPA TUTOIA BANK　Architect : Siegbert Zanettini　96
バネスパ・ツトイア銀行　設計：シーギベルチ・ザネチーニ

HOSPITAL FOR THE HANDICAPPED　Architect : João F. Lima　98
身体障害者のための病院　設計：ジョアオ・フィウゲイラス・リーマ

ADMINISTRATIVE CENTER OF BAHIA　Architect : Joao F. Lima　102
バイーア州行政センター　設計：ジョアオ・フィウゲイラス・リーマ

CAB CHAPEL　Architect : Joao F. Lima　107
CABチャペル　設計：ジョアオ・フィウゲイラス・リーマ

MIGUEL DE CERVANTES HIGH SCHOOL　Architect : Rino Levi　112
ミゲウ・デ・セルバンテス校　設計：リーノ・レーヴィ

CAETANO DE CAMPOS TRAINING SCHOOL　Architects : Croce, Aflalo & Gasperini　116
カエターノ・デ・カンポス校　設計：クロッチェ，アフラーロ & ガスペリーニ

CEESP TRADENTES BANK　Architects : Croce, Aflalo & Gasperini　119
セエスビ・チラデンテス銀行　設計：クロッチェ，アフラーロ & ガスペリーニ

IGUATEMI BUILDING　Architects : Croce, Aflalo & Gasperini　122
イグアテミー・ビルディング　設計：クロッチェ，アフラーロ & ガスペリーニ

CAMPOS DO JORDAO HALL　Architects : Croce, Aflalo & Gasperini　124
カンポス・ド・ジョルドン・ホール　設計：クロッチェ，アフラーロ & ガスペリーニ

SIGRIST RESIDENCE　Architect : Eduardo de Almeida　126
シーグリスチ邸　設計：エドゥアルド・デ・アウメイダ

ALMEIDA RESIDENCE　Architect : Eduardo de Almeida　128
アウメイダ邸　設計：エドゥアルド・デ・アウメイダ

DEFINE RESIDENCE　Architect : Eduardo de Almeida　131
デファイネ邸　設計：エドゥアルド・デ・アウメイダ

ANNEX FOR THE LEGISLATIVE ASSEMBLY　Architects : Ramalho, Oba & Zamoner　134
下院議会別館　設計：ラマーリョ，オオバ & ザモネール

PERNAMBUCO EXPO CENTER　Architects : Ramalho, Oba & Zamoner　137
ベルナンブーコ・エクスポ・センター　設計：ラマーリョ，オオバ & ザモネール

TERRAFOTO HEADQUARTERS　Architects : Ramalho, Oba & Zamoner　140
テラフォト本社　設計：ラマーリョ，オオバ & ザモネール

ACARPA HEADQUARTERS　Architect : Luiz Forte Netto　142
アカルパ本部　設計：ルイス・フォルテ・ネット

ERPLAN HEADQUARTERS　Architects : Lima, Machado, Matsuzawa & Yamaki　146
エルプラン本部　設計：リーマ，マシャード，マツザワ & ヤマキ

PROCESS
: Architecture

Number 17

Publisher
Bunji Murotani

Editor in charge
Humberto Yamaki

Production Editor
Michiko Sakae

Cover Design
Takashi Marumo

Advisors
Nader Ardalan, *Teheran*
Jonathan Barnett, *New York*
Craig Ellwood, *Los Angeles*
R. Buckminster Fuller, *Philadelphia*
Bill N. Lacy, *New York*
David Lewis, *Pittsburgh*
Fumihiko Maki, *Tokyo*
Isamu Noguchi, *New York*
Cesar Pelli, *New Haven*
Bernard Rudofsky, *Malaga*
Peter Smithson, *London*

Copyright © August 1980 by Process
Architecture Publishing Co., Ltd.,
Tokyo, Japan.
All right reserved.

Distribution in U.S.A. and Canada
Eastview Editions, Inc.
Box 783
Westfield, New Jersey 07091, U.S.A.
Tel : (201)233-0474

Process : Architecture is published by
Process Architecture Publishing Co.,
Ltd., Tokyo, and Printed in Japan by
Kyodo Printing Co., Ltd., Tokyo.

Executive and Editorial
3-1-3 Koishikawa, Bunkyo-ku, Tokyo,
Japan.
Tel : (03)816-1695·1696

Logotype Design
Aijiro Wakita

Translator
Melissa Mukai

Cover : Julio de Mesquita Filio Hospital (see p.48)
Back Cover : CECAP Taubate Housing (see p.54)

ISBN 0-89860-043-X

編集言

この特集号は今日のブラジルにおける建築の状況を紹介する。最近の建築表現を様々な角度から眺め,全体的な視点を提供するという基準のもとに各作品は選ばれている。ここに示された各々の計画案は,さまざまな建物の内容のデザインを広範囲にわたって含んでいる。また紙面の都合により一部の作品を割愛したが,その作業は困難をきわめた。

最近出版された本ではほとんど触れられることのなかったブラジル建築の新鮮なイメージを提供するのが本書の目的である。

工業あるいは経済開発という点だけではなく人間の集まりという点においても,ブラジルは対照に富んだ国である。設計の方向が多様なのは,アマゾンの多雨地帯から非常に雨の少ない北東地域,そして時には雪も降る南部地域にいたる多彩な地理的気候的条件を誇る面積330万平方マイルの広大な国土によるところが大きい。

建築形態の独創性と自由奔放さ,そして豊富な土着的語法やポルトガル・バロックの伝統に根ざした表現方法などによってブラジルは世界の注目を集めてきた。

ブラジル建築はその創設期より独自の道を歩みながら変化し発展してきた。そして時には批判にさらされまたある時は喝采をもって迎えられたのである。J・ゲーデスはその過程について次のように述べたことがある。「ブラジル建築の目的は美の古典的形を見つけ出すことではなく,厳しい意識的な努力の結果得られる美を求めることである」。現在のブラジル建築がおかれている真の状態を明白に表わす,対立した時には矛盾する態度から,このような作品群が生み出されている。作品解説の中で用いられるメタファーは,ブラジルの建築関係の文章で流行しているいいまわしの典型である。

上田篤教授による序文はブラジルの空間や環境の意味を伝えている。そしてその後にカルロス・レーモス氏が1970年までのブラジル建築の歴史を紹介する文章を寄せている。そして,ブラジルのデザイン空間に対する多様な全体像を示す「ブラジル——建築のカレイドスコープ」が収載されている。

最後に,この特集号の編集を助けてくださった多くの方々,そしてこの号に登場していただいた建築家たち,特に全体の方針について助言を承った建築家の加藤晃規氏に感謝の意を表したい。

(ウンベルト八巻)

Editorial

This special issue introduces the architectural scene in Brazil today. The works were selected under criteria designed to offer a global view of current architectural expression from different angles. The projects presented cover a wide range of building types and designs, and the selection of works necessitated by space limitations was very difficult.

A renewed image of Brazilian architecture is offered here as recent books dealing with the subject are rare.

Brazil is a country of contrasts not only in terms of technological and economic development but of human groups as well. The diversity of design trends is induced in part by the country's huge physical area, 3.3 million square miles, boasting a wide variety of geographical and climatic conditions, from the Amazon rain forest to the semi-arid northeast and the occasionally snowy south.

Brazil has attracted worldwide attention with the originality and freedom of its architectural forms and with a language rich in native idiom and modes of expression related to the Portugese Baroque tradition.

Since its pioneer days, Brazilian architecture has changed and developed in its own way, criticized by some and acclaimed by others. J. Guedes has said of the process that "its intent is not a search for a classic form of beauty, but instead for beauty as the result of conscious and rigorous effort." This group of works results from an antagonistic and sometimes contradictory attitude that defines the real state of today's architecture in Brazil. The metaphors used in the accompanying text are typical of current usage in Brazil's architectural writings.

An introductory note by Professor Atsushi Ueda imparts a sense of Brazil's space and environment, after which Professor Carlos Lemos introduces the history of Brazilian architecture to 1970. A kaleidoscope of Brazilian architecture follows, offering a diverse panorama of designed space in Brazil.

Finally, I would like here to express my thanks to the many people who helped compile this issue, to thearchitects noted elsewhere herein, and especially to Mr. Akinori Kato, architect, for his comments on general orientation.
(Humberto Yamaki)

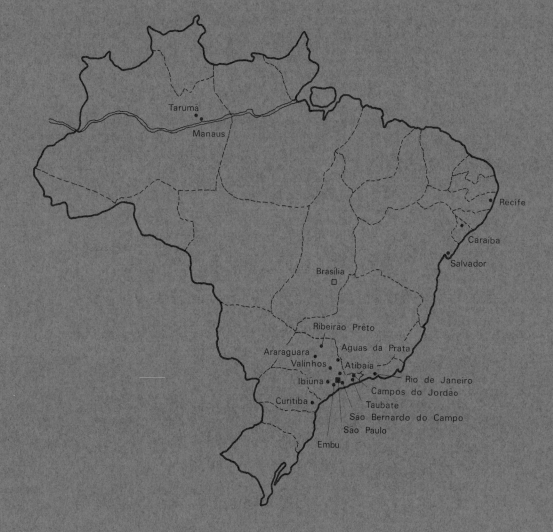

ウンベルト・八巻
1952年サンパウロに生まれる。1972年から'76年にかけて,いくつかの建築事務所で働く。1976年サンパウロ大学建築・都市計画科卒業。同年エルプラン本部の設計競技にチームで入賞。1977年から78年まで,日本政府の奨学金を受けて京都大学工学部建築学科の研究生となる。1978年,黒川紀章建築・都市設計事務所のベイヤー・デザイン設計競技入賞者チームのメンバーとなる。1979年から日本政府の奨学金を受けて,大阪大学環境工学科大学院在学。

HUMBERTO YAMAKI
Born in Sao Paulo, Brasil. on 1952 From 1972 to '76, Works at Various architectural offices and private atelier. Graduated from School of Architecture and Urbanism, University of Sao Paulo, Brasil. on 1976. Winner entry in the ERPLAN RIBEIRAO PRETO Design Competition(team) on 1976. From 1977 to 1978, research at Kyoto University, Faculty of Engineering, Dept. of Architecture, receiving Japanese Goverment Fellowship. 1978, Member of Bayer Design Competition Winner Team at Kisho Kurokawa, architect & associates. From 1979~, Research at Osaka University, Dept. of Environmental Engineering receiving Japanese Government Fellowship.

IMPRESSIVE SCENE OF BRASILIA
by Atsushi Ueda

ブラジリアの印象
上田篤

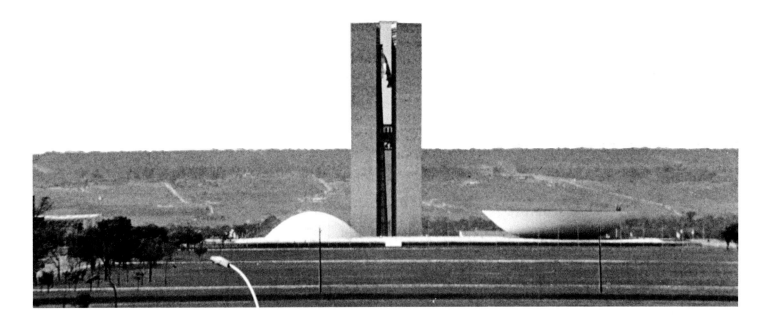

夜のバスの窓に，ボンヤリとジャンボの機首がうつる．車がカーブをきるたびに，つぎつぎとことなった航空会社のマークの機首が窓面にあらわれては消えあらわれては消える．それ以外，空港はまっくら，バスのなかもまっくら．乗客はだれも黙して語らない．このまま，地底の闇のなかへすいこまれていってもふしぎではないような，そんな錯覚をおぼえる．

いつものような羽田の国際線での旅立ちの風景ではあるが，こんどはわたしにとってちょっとなにかしら，勝手がちがうようだ．

オズという国がある．童話にでてくるとおくはるかな不思議の国である．いまのこの旅立ちは，わたしにとって，オズへとむかう第一歩なのである．なにしろ，1個の飛行機にのって26時間あまりのたったそれだけで地球の表面をかっきり半周して，日本の真裏に到着するのだ．そこは11月のいま，初夏である．リオの海

Staring blankly out the window of a bus one night, the nose of a jumbo jet appeared before my eyes. Every time the bus made a turn, the logo of various airlines rose and faded in the pane. Aside from that, the airport road was pitch black and inside the bus, too, was dark. None of the passengers spoke. I remember feeling that it wouldn't seem at all out of the ordinary to be suddenly sucked into the center of the earth. It was the same old start of a trip to Haneda (International Airport), but this time I felt somehow awkward.

There is a country called Oz in children's stories; it's a strange land far away. For me, this was the first step on a trip to Oz. In a little over 26 hours, one airplane would describe a semi-circle in flight and land on the other side of the world. It was February, the beginning of summer there. Rio's beaches would be full of girls in bikinis and tongas. In São Paulo, red, yellow, green, blue and purple cotton shirts would strike a fine contrast on white, black and brown skins as the wearers packed the streets, dancing.

The trip to Brasilia was interesting. The one o'clock bus from São Paulo heads due north for 16 hours, seven or eight of which

岸通りにはビキニや，あのタンガとよばれる優雅な女性用の水着があふれていることであろう．サンパウロの街では，赤・黄・緑・青・紫などのコットン・シャツが，白い素肌，黒い素肌，小麦色の素肌などにピッタリと密着して乱舞していることだろう．

＊

ブラジリアへの陸路からのアプローチもまた，おもしろい．サンパウロを午後1時にたったバスは，真北へむかって，飛ばしに飛ばして16時間．暗黒のなかを走ってからさえ7,8時間．はじめのうちこそときたま町もあり，畠もあったが，日が暮れてからは，1軒家の灯さえみること稀になり，いったいこの先に何があるのだろうと思われるような闇の中を一途に北上して，ようやく東の空がかすかに白みはじめたかにみえる午前5時ごろになって，前方に一条の光の線がみえてきた．やがてそれはだんだん大きくなり，バスの両側の窓にも等分に拡がる大きさに成長する．ふしぎなことに立体感はまったくない．どこまでも横にひろがる一条の線，さながらそれは光の地平線である．光平線とでもよぶべきか．ブラジリアはブラジル中央高原のまったく何もないセラードのなかで，陸路でアプローチするものにそういうあらわれ方をする町なのである．

＊

けさはめずらしくおそくまでねていた．時計はすでに，9時半をさしている．朝日がカーテンのわずかな隙間からもれてきて，へ

やのなかはボンヤリとうすあかるい．そしてしずかだ．いつも朝7時にはじまる建築工事の物音もきこえてこない．自動車のエンジンの音も，タイヤがコンクリートをきしる音も，きょうはまばらだ．ただかすかに，とおくのほうで人の声がする．それもたくさんの人声が．

カーテンをあける．けさの空は，まぶしいくらいの青空．ブラジリアにきてはじめてのことだ．そう，わたしはまだブラジリアにいる．きょうで7日目．その6日間は，毎日雨だった．きょうは久しぶりにいい天気だ．

朝食をすませて半袖シャツ1枚になって，外に出る．遠く声がする方へ向って，ホテルから西へ10分ほど歩いたところに，テレビ塔がたっている．トーレという個有名詞でよばれ，ブラジリアのランドマークのひとつになっている．その下に日曜市が開かれている．日曜の朝の空気を破る声の発生源はじつはこれなのだ．しかし，20分ほどで市を丹念に2周してまわると，もうあとはすることがない．ひとつノビをしてまわりの景色をながめる．いやでも目に入ってくるのが，例のお碗をひろげたのとふせたのとからなるブラジル国民議会の三権広場だ．そのほかは，豆腐をきったような四角い建物の，それこそ無限の連続．計画的といえば計画的．単調といえば単調．だからニーマイヤーの設計になる三権広場以外，目に入らないのも当然である．そして，そちらの方へと，自然に足がむいてゆくのもいたしかたない．もっとも足が向

are consumed in night. At first, of course, there are fields and towns, but when night falls it becomes rare to see a light in a window, and one wonders just what lies ahead as the bus speeds through the gloom. At last some white steals faintly into the eastern sky, around five o'clock in the morning, and then a single beam of light. As that gradually gets bigger, the windows of both sides of the bus grow with it. Strangely, it has no volume. That single ray spreads everywhere, as if it had become the skyline, or perhaps it should be called the lightline. Taking the overland approach, Brasilia appears to be in the middle of nowhere on Brazil's central plateau.

One morning I slept unusually late. My watch already said nine-thirty. The morning sun slipped through a crack in the curtains, filling the room with a thin light. It was quiet. I hadn't heard the construction noise that always began at seven. The sounds of car engines and tires hitting the pavement was scattered. I heard only people's voices in the distance; it sounded like a lot of people.

I opened the curtains; the morning sky was a bright blue. This was the first time I had been to Brasilia. Yes, I was still in Brasilia; this was my seventh day. It rained on each of the previous six days; now we finally had some good weather. I finished my breakfast, put on a shortsleeved shirt and went out, heading in the direction of those voices.

There is a television tower about a ten minute walk west of the hotel. Called simply Tôrre, it is one of Brasilia's landmarks. I heard the Sunday market at the foot of the tower – that was the source of the voices that broke the Sunday morning air. But a walk around the city takes 20 minutes, and aside from that there is nothing to do. I stretched and looked at the surrounding scenery.

The eye cannot avoid the governmental plaza in front of Brazil's parliament, itself shaped like two bowls, one up and one down. Beyond that are endless blocks of square buildings. It looks very "planned," and very monotonous. It is not surprising, perhaps, that nothing but Niemeyer's governmental plaza strikes the eye here. One can't help but turn in its direction, yet, even as doing so, it's hard to guess how many miles off it is. Here in Brasilia one's visual sense of distance is driven mad. Something may look close but actually be far away, or look distant and

いたとしても，遠くにかすかにみえる三権広場まで，何キロある
か，ちょっと見当もつかない．ここブラジリアでは，すべての視
覚的距離感はくるわされる．近いとおもえば遠く，遠いとおもえ
ば意外に近いこともある．だがおよそ幅200メートルぐらいはあ
るかとおもわれる，それこそ，真一直線に三権広場へと向う広い
芝生道は，日曜の散歩にはまことに快適である．そこここに，赤
や白や紫の花が咲いている．名前のわからないのが残念である．
両側の建物はホテル街や商業街から，やがて鋼鉄のようにとぎす
まされたコンクリートとガラスの官庁街へとかわってゆく．その
建物の妻壁のひとつひとつに官庁の名前が書かれている．アルフ
ァベットをたどりつつ，それをよんでゆくのも楽しい．鉱山・エ
ネルギー省，教育省，空軍省……．なかには意味のわからないも
のもあるが．だが，これほど官庁街が近接して計画的にわかりや
すく配置されているのも，ちょっと例がない．この一群の官庁街
をみていると，この空間配置からこの国に，かつてなかった「官
僚制」というものが，いまようやく芽生えてくる可能性もあるの
ではないか，とおもわれてくる．

＊

ブラジリアは，いうところの「人間無視」の街である．歩行者に
対しては何の処置もなされていないといってもよい．ブラジリア
中に満足な歩道は1本もないのである．いま歩いてきた幅200メ
ートルの芝生道にも歩道らしきものは何もない．だがそれゆえに，

歩行者には危険とひきかえにではあるが，無限の可能性がある．
思いがけない空間の接近がある．

ブラジリアは冷たい街だが，なまじ人間にこびないその冷たさ
が何ともいえず好ましくみえることもあるものだ．

私は上半身裸になってベンチの上に寝ころがった．紫外線のつ
よい太陽が肌を射る．サングラスにもまばゆい青空．そしてはた
めくブラジル国旗．それは，高さ15メートル，幅25メートルぐら
いはある．ビルひとつ分ぐらいの大きさである．

みるともなしにその国旗をみていて，私はそこに書かれている
字を追った．空中7，80メートルの高さにあるためか強い風にはた
めいて，なかなかそのスペル全部がよみとれない．長いことかか
ってやっと全部よみとれた．それは，ORDEM E PROGRESSO
と書かれてあった．「秩序と進歩」である．

私はこの時はじめてブラジル国旗にかかれている文字をよんだ
のである．

上田篤：大阪大学教授．

really be near at hand.

Running in a straight line toward the governmental plaza is
an avenue of grassy lawn, about 200 meters in width; it makes
for a truly comfortable Sunday stroll. Here and there are flowers
of red, blue, and purple – I wish I knew their names. Lining
either side of the avenue are hotels and stores which farther along
give way to governmental buildings of concrete and glass stretched over steel frames. At the top of each is written the name of
the agency it houses. I enjoyed just letting my eyes follow the
line of letters as I read: the Ministry of Mines and Energy, Ministry of Education, Ministry of the Air Force, and some whose
names I couldn't fathom. It's unprecedented for so many min-
istries to be located by plan so close together. Looking at this
group of them, I wonder if the seeds of bureacracy aren't planted
here.

Brasilia denies the existence of people. Nothing is provided
for the pedestrian. There is not a single satisfactory walkway.
Even on this 200-meter wide avenue of lawn there is no sort of
footpath. Yet, while this situation invites dangers for the pedestrian, it is full of possibilities. Its spatial quality is unexpected.

Brasilia is a cold town, but that very aloofness has its own
appeal. I took off my shirt and lay down on a bench. The strong
sun heat down on my skin and the blue sky glared through my
sunglasses. The Brazilian flag fluttered in the wind; about 15 by
25 meters in size, it was almost as big as one of those buildings.

Staring at the flag, my eyes followed the letters. I could hardly
read them, either due to the strong wind or the fact that they
were 70 or 80 meters above me. I finally did make them out –
the flag reads, *ordem e progresso*, order and progress. That was
the first time I'd read the flag's motto.

Atsushi Ueda : Professor, Faculty of Environmental Engineering, Osaka University.

NOTES ON THE MODERN BRAZILIAN ARCHITECTURE
by Carlos A. C. Lemos

現代ブラジル建築概観　　カルロス・A・C・レーモス

産業革命によって建設技術の分野に急激な変化をこうむったヨーロッパ以外の諸国におけると同様に，ブラジルにおいても世紀末頃の技術者たちの創意に満ちた働きぶりは見過されてきた．新しい技術に対する美学は，その時代に行われていた伝統的な教育システムの中で否定されたのである．

近代建築運動の初期の頃にはいわゆる「正統派」を自認する建築家たちは新しい技術を採り入れはしたが，あたかもそれが真の建築であると正式に認められていたかのように，確かな学識に基づくファサードを用いて構造体をおおい隠したのであった．

現代ブラジル建築の先駆者となり新技術を紹介した幾人かの技術者と知られざる建築家たちがいたが，彼等の作品は評価されることなく終り，そしてそのうちの多くが，ひっきりなしに行われた都市再開発のおかげで取り壊されてし

In Brazil, as elsewhere outside of Europe where the Industrial Revolution caused a sudden change in the technology of construction, the inventive effort of engineers and technicians at the turn of the century passed unnoticed. The aesthetic of the new technology was not valued by the traditional academic training system of the time.

At the beginning of the modern movement the "official" architects employed the new technology but concealed the structural systems to maintain a facade of proper eruditeness, such as was officially recognized as true architecture.

There were some engineers and anonymous architects, pioneers of modern Brazilian architecture, who displayed the new technology, but their work went unappreciated and much of it was destroyed by the incressant efforts of urban renewal, especially in São Paulo, Rio de Janiero, and Belo Horizonte.

The question of structural system is most important as it is the fundamental determinant of the architectural concept, more so than any other factor considered in a contemporary view of architecture, more, even, than the aesthetic intention.

①② Mairinque Station, São Paulo, c. 1907 by V. Dubugras

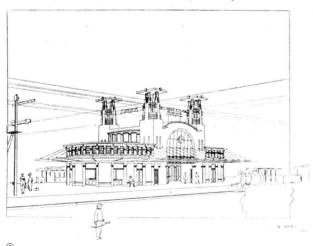

まった．それは特に，サンパウロ，リオデジャネイロ，ベーロ・オリゾンテにおいて激しいものであった．

構造システムの問題は，建築の今日的な視点において考慮される他の要因より，さらには美学上の意図よりも，建築概念の基本的な決定要因として，大変重要なものである．現在の生活に適した建築は，新しい技術を用いることによってはじめて実現できる．

ブラジルでも他の多くの国々と同様，現代の先駆者たちの創り出した作品は建築としてよりも工学的成果として位置づけられてきた．彼らは忘れ去られ，そして現代建築運動といえば自分たちの現代性を十分に意識しそれを自慢にさえしていた建築家だけを連想するのである．現代的であるということは，単に他のものから異なっていて，繰り返しをしないことであると，ある人たちは考えていた．彼らの中には，ネオ・コロニアルの大家たちも含まれていた．

ネオ・コロニアルはブラジルにおける最後の折衷主義的な建築運動で，支配者階級の国粋主義者的な反応として生まれた．

今世紀の初頭，リオデジャネイロでは，ペレイラ・パーソス知事の断行した事業に対し，懸念と驚きの声があがっていた．彼は堂々とした「セントラル・アベニュー」と呼ばれる目抜き通りと，他にもいくつかの通りを開通させた．それらはやがて，折衷主義的な工法という昔ながらの方法でできあがった．この仕事は主にポルトガル人を中心とする熟練した移民の職人たちによって達成された．

このような傾向はサンパウロでも同様であり，都市の表情は移民の人々の手によってぬりかえられてしまったのである．この地の経済はコーヒー産業の出現に支えられ繁栄した．この両都市はブエノス・アイレスのように急速にヨーロッパ的な雰囲気を帯び，やがて南アメリカの中心都市と呼ばれるようになった．

このような折衷主義に対する反発はサンパウロ市を中心に起り，特にコーヒー産業を独占し政治を牛耳っていた伝統的な社会から離れて仕事をしていた人々の間で，それは顕著であった．

ポルトガルから亡命してきたリカルド・セベーロは，1914年リオデジャネイロで行われた独立記念100年祭においてその特色となった新鮮さを，ネオ・コロニアル様式に導入した．サンパウロにおいては，新進気鋭のモダニストたちによって現代美術週間 (the Modern Art Week) が1922年に組織された．

この運動に参加した建築家でブラジル人は一

Only a new technology can result in an architecture compatible with the order of life today.

The pioneers of the contemporary era in Brazil as elsewhere produced work which was recognized more as engineering than as architecture. They are forgotten and modern movements are associated with those architects who were highly conscious of, even boastful of, their modernity. Some thought that to be modern was simply to be different from others, never to repeat oneself. Among them were the masters of the Neo-Colonial.

The Neo-Colonial was the last eclectic Brazilian movement and arose as a nationalist reaction of the dominating class.

At the beginning of this century, Rio de Janeiro watched the intervention of Prefect Pereira Passos in the city with fear and amazement. He opened the large Central Avenue and other streets soon to be defined by the antiquated courses of Eclectic construction. The work was done by skilled immigrant craftsmen, mainly the Portuguese.

The same trend occurred in São Paulo, where the immigrants transformed the face of the city. The economy there flourished with the emergence of the coffee industry. Both cities rapidly assumed a European air, like Buenos Aires, then considered the capital of South America.

A reaction to this eclecticism arose in São Paulo, especially among those who practiced apart from the traditional society which had become engrossed in coffee and politics.

In 1914, Ricardo Severo, a Portugese exile, brought to the Neo-Colonial style the freshness that characterized the Centenary Commemoration of Independence in Rio de Janeiro. In São Paulo, young modernists organized the Modern Art Week of 1922.

It should be noted that no architects participating in this movement were Brazilian, indicating that the new style was more easily accepted from outside than a reform growing from the cultural heart of the nation. The ideas of Ricardo Severo bore fruit in the offices of Spanish Antonio Garcia Moya, Polish Jorg Pryzenbel and French-Argentine Victor Dubugras, who saw acceptability and com-

③ Esther Building, São Paulo, 1937 by A. V. Brazil

④ Ministry of Education Building, Rio de Janeiro, 1936 by Lucio Costa & others

⑤ Brazilian Press Association, Rio de Janeiro, 1936, M. M. M. Roberto

人もいなかった．これは，人々は新しい様式については，自国の文化に深くかかわりそこから徐々に生まれてきたものよりも，国の外から入ってきたものの方を容易に受け入れたということを示しており，このことは記憶にとどめておくべきである．リカルド・セベーロの考えは，スペイン人のアントニオ・ガルシーア・モーヤ，ポーランド人のジョルジェ・プリゼンベウそしてフランス系アルゼンチン人のヴィクトル・ドゥブグラスの事務所において実を結んだ．彼らは，古い植民地時代の建築は改良してゆく余地があり，かつそれによって経済的な利益があがることを見ぬいていた．

現代美術週間の主催者たちを含め，彼らはすべて年若く，建築における真のモダニズムを，あるいは新しい時代に合致する新しい表現を生み出すことを夢見ていた．

ブラジル経済の中でも工業部門は合理的な現代建築が必要とする新しい技術を維持していくだけの設備を備えていなかった．ガラス，セメント，鉄，屋根葺き材，パイプ，配管設備，衛生設備等，大部分の材料は輸入にたよっており，高価であった．木材と木構造材は第一次大戦までは北欧とスラブ諸国の松が使われていた．

最初に実現された現代建築の考え方は，現実に即したものというよりはむしろ理論が先行したものであった．建築的改革の最初の記録は，1925年のリオデジャネイロの新聞記事に見い出すことができる．その記事は，サンパウロ市に住んでいるグレゴリ・ワシャービシッキというロシア人の建築家によって書かれたものであり，彼は以前にもイタリア系の新聞に同じ内容の記事を発表したことがあった．

ワシャービシッキはコルビュジエによって提案された自由な立面と平面を実現するのに必要な材料が不足しているにもかかわらず，モダニスト的な住宅を建設した．彼は新しい建築の考え方はどんなものであるか，ということを紹介したのであった．

現代の合理主義的な建築は1930年代に確立された．ワシャービシッキのマニフェストと30年代に起きた革命の間に生じたいくつかの決定的な出来事によって来るべき時代の新しい考え方が大きく前進した．その第1番目は，ルチオ・コスタがネオ・コロニアリズムからモダニズムへと転身を計ったことであり，第2番目はリオデジャネイロとサンパウロにおける会議に出席するため，ル・コルビュジエがブラジルを訪れたことである．これらは新しい美学が公認される上で決定的な影響を及ぼした．

国立美術学校の校長としてルチオ・コスタが指名されたことは非常に重要なことであった．

mercial profit in the reform of the old Colonial-era architecture.

All of them, including the organizors of the Modern Art Week, were young modern men hoping to produce a true architectural modernism, a new expression consistent with the new era.

The Brazilian economy, especially the industrial sector, did not have the facilities to support the new technology of a rational modern architecture. Most materials were imported and expensive — glass, cement, iron, roofing tiles, pipe, plumbing and sanitary equipment. Until World War I, lumber and wooden structures were constructed of Nordic and Slav pine.

The first modern ideas to be realized were more theoretical than practical. The first record of an architectural reform is found in a Rio de Janeiro newspaper of 1925. The article was written by a Russian architect named Gregory Warchavchick living in São Paulo, where he had previously dealt with this matter in an Italian colony newspaper.

Warchavchick constructed modernist houses although he was limited in the materials necessary for the free facades and terraces proposed by Le Corbusier. He introduced the ideas of a new architecture.

Modern rational architecture was defined in the 1930s. Between the manifesto of Warchavchick and the Revolution of the Thirties, some decisive events favored the growth of new ideas in the years to come: first, the conversion of the architect Lucio Costa from Neo-Colonialism to Modernism; and second, Le Corbusier's visit to Brazil, at conferences in Rio de Janeiro and São Paulo. These were decisive influences in the adoption of the new aesthetic.

The nomination of Lucio Costa as a Director of the National School of Fine Arts was very important. He held the post for only a short period due to the reaction of other professors to his innovative approach. But during that time students' ideas were influenced by the information he provided regarding the new aesthetic

⑥⑦ Santos Dumont Airpot, Rio de Janeiro, 1937−1944 by M. M. M. Roberto

⑥

⑦

彼のものごとに対する取り組み方は革新的でありそれによって他の教授たちの反感を買ったため，彼がこの地位についていたのはほんの短い間であった．しかしながらこの短期間の間に，学生たちの考え方は，彼の用意した新しい美学的方向性に関する情報によって大きな影響をうけた．

30年代の中頃にリオデジャネイロに建設されたいくつかの建物は，都市景観に対して大きな衝撃力を持つものであった．そして意外なことにそれらの建物は大衆からも大いに歓迎されたのである．

ブラジル新聞協会（ＡＢＩ）の建物を決める設計競技において，Ｍ・Ｍ・Ｍ・ロベルト兄弟がコンクリート製の固定ブリーズソレーユを用いたデザインで入選を果たした．また飛行艇の発着所を内容の一部として含む設計競技では，アチーリオ・コスタが新しい理論に従ったデザインを発表して賞を獲得した．

しかしその中でももっとも重要な計画はルチオ・コスタに率いられた前衛建築家たちが，ル・コルビュジエの助言を得ながら設計した，リオデジャネイロにある教育健康省の建物であった．設計競技においては当初，アール・デコの考え方に基づく案が入選したが，新しいものを十分に学んでいた当時の教育相，グスターボ・カパネマは新しい設計を提案したのであった．この計画のために，ル・コルビュジエはブラジルを2度にわたって訪れている．

教育健康省の計画に携わった設計チームは建物の完成後に解散したが，そこに参加した建築家たちは自分たちのオフィスを開設して新しい考え方をさらに推し進めた．リオデジャネイロにおける現代建築は強烈で革新的な衝撃を受けたのである．その中の中心となった方向性はミースやグロピウスらの作品に基づく機能主義であった．

第2次世界大戦中は建設物資の輸入が困難となり，また国内の材料さえも不足しがちであったため，建築家はさらに地域に密着した表現を見付け出さねばならなかった．こうした仕事の成果は，ニューヨークの近代美術館で開かれた「Brazil Builds」と題したブラジル建築の展覧会で広く一般に認められた．

柔軟性を表現しようとする，オスカー・ニーマイヤーの作品の意図は，国際的にも認められた．自由な形態を生み出す力は鉄筋コンクリートの潜在的可能性の一つであり，それは合理主義から生み出された作品，すなわちかちっとした左右対称の幾何学的形態を持つ傑作とはまったく異なったものであった．

40年代に入って，曲線や波状の線が用いられるようになると，形の構成に対する固定的な価

trend.

In the mid-Thirties, some buildings constructed in Rio de Janeiro had a strong impact on the cityscape and received an unexpectedly good reception from the public.

The competition for the Brazilian Press Association building (ABI) was won by M.M.M. Roberto Brothers with a design of fixed reinforced concrete brise-soleil. Another competition involving a terminal for seaplanes was won by Atilio Costa with a design conforming to the new theories.

But the most important project was the Ministry of Education and Health in Rio de Janeiro, designed by vanguard architects led by Lucio Costa with the advice of Le Corbusier. The competition was originally won by an Art Deco concept but the modern-leaning Minister of Education, Gustavo Capanema, submitted a new design. Le Corbusier visited Brazil a second time on behalf of this project.

The design team for the Ministry of Education project dispersed after its completion, with each architect advancing new ideas in his own office. Modern architecture in Rio de Janeiro received a great innovative impulse. The main orientation was functionalism, based on the works of Mies and Gropius, among others.

During World War II, architects, limited by the difficulty of importing construction materials and by the scarcity of even local materials, were forced to find a more local expression. Their success was recognized by the New York Museum of Modern Art in an exhibition of Brazilian architecture entitled "Brazil Builds."

International acknowledgment identified the emerging plasticity of the works of Oscar Niemeyer. The potential of reinforced concrete lay in its capacity for free forms, unlike the creations of rationalism which were masterpieces of sharp, symmetrical geometric volumes.

In the Forties, the liberation from these rigid values and rules of composi-

⑧ Hidroplane Station, Rio de Janeiro, 1938 by Attilio Correia Lima

⑨ Casino, Pampulha, 1942 by O. Niemeyer

値や規則が打ち破られ，バロックに似た合成的な空間が生み出された．また同じことが新しい表現を誤解している人々によって批判されたのである．

この10年間はコルビュジエによって提案された概念を咀嚼する時期であった．それは新しい意味論上の要素からなるまったく別の言葉で表現されていた．オスカー・ニーマイヤーの建築は柔軟で詩情に富むパンプーリャから始まった．

現代ブラジル建築の創設期にはニーマイヤーの作品だけでなくミースやグロピウスの作品が想像力の源泉となった．ライトの考え方もサンパウロのリーノ・レーヴィやリオデジャネイロのジョルジェ・モレイラを含む建築家たちの間に信奉者を生み出した．1940年代には異なった系統の建築学校が設立され，それは今日に至るまで工学系の学校を中で補足するプログラムとなってきた．サンパウロ市に建てられた建物の性格は，これらの学校と第2次大戦後にブラジルへ移民してきた建築家たちに負うところが大きい．リーノ・レーヴィの他にも，彼と同じく急速にふくれあがった都市，すなわちサンパウロで働いていたビラノーバ・アルチーガスとオスヴァルド・ブラチケにも言及しておくべきであろう．彼らは折衷主義にもとづく組積建築の代りに鉄筋コンクリートの建築を設計したのであった．

コミュニケーションが容易になりそのスピードがあがって消費が増大するようになると，必然的に二つの動きは一つの運動へと収束した．

ブラジリアの計画からうかがえるように，ニーマイヤーはニーマイヤーであり続けた．彼の作品は多くの若い建築家たちに影響を与えた．彼らの作品は単なる模倣にすぎることなく巨匠の造形力に富んだ作品と同じような柔軟な内容を持っている．

自由な形態を支持する人もまた形式主義を支持する人も，鉄筋コンクリートはそれまで用いられていたより以上に，さらにどんな形にもなり得る可能性を秘めているとの結論を下した．それは合理的な解決策を生み出すことができると同時に建築空間を形成する上で主要な要素となるのだ．

現場打ちの打放しコンクリートは，現代ブラジル建築として知られているものの内容を生み出してきたし，これからもそれを特徴づけて行くことだろう．

カルロス・A・C・レーモス：建築家，画家，サンパウロ大学教授．

tion were induced by the instruction of curved and sinuous lines, with resultant spaces similar to those of the Baroque. This similarity was criticised by those misunderstanding the new expression.

This decade was a period of digestion of Le Corbusier's concepts, expressed in a new language of novel semantic elements. The architecture of Oscar Niemeyer began with Pampulha, plastic and lyrical.

The beginning of modern Brazilian architecture found inspiration in Niemeyer's work and that of Mies and Gropius. Wright's theories, too, had a few adherents, including Rino Levi in São Paulo and Jorge Moreira in Rio de Janeiro.

In the 1940s, separate schools of architecture, which until this time had been complementary pograms within schools of engineering, were established. São Paulo owes the character of its architecture to these schools and to the architects who emigrated to Brazil after World War II. Besides Rino Levi, we should mention Villanova Artigas and Oswaldo Bratke who were also working in the rapidly growing city. They substituted reinforced concrete for the masonry buildings of Eclecticism.

Inevitably, the two pioneering trends melded into a single movement with the increased ease and speed of communications and the growth of consumerism.

Niemeyer continued as Niemeyer, as demonstrated at Brasilia. His work influenced many young architects whose works are not merely imitations, but have plastic conclusions similar to those of the master. The proponents of both free form and formalism concluded that reinforced concrete had more ductile potential than was being used. It could permit a rational solution and, at the same time, be a major component of architectural space.

Poured-in-place concrete, all exposed, has produced and continues to characterize what is known as modern Brazilian architecture.

Carlos Alberto Cerqueira Lemos : Architect, Painter, Professor of the school of Architecture and Urbanism, University of São Paulo.

⑩⑪ San Francisco Chapel, Pampulha, 1943 by O.Niemeyer

⑩

⑪

O. ニーマイヤーのスケッチから　　SKETCHES BY OSCAR NIEMEYER

O. Niemeyer

　ブラジリアの記念碑的な建築の設計者として広く名を知られているオスカー・ニーマイヤーは，ブラジル近代建築における中心的人物である．彼は，今年で73歳を数えるが，今なお積極的な活動を続けており，その作品は世界各地に数多くつくられている．

　ニーマイヤーの作品では曲線がよく用いられ，その造形は感覚的ともいえるものであるが，それは，建築の分野が芸術としてとりあつかわれる，ブラジル的な建築的思想を反映している．ここでは，70年代の作品のいくつかを，彼自身のスケッチによって紹介する．

　スケッチは，最終的プレゼンテーションとしては一般にあまり利用されない．しかし，ニーマイヤーの空間を表現するにはこの方法が最も適していると思われる．このスケッチによる表現ということ自体，ニーマイヤーから，学ぶべきことのひとつであるともいえよう．

これらのスケッチは，彼自身が編集している雑誌 MÓDULO, Revista de Arquitetura Arte, e Cultura から提供されたものである．ニーマイヤー氏には，多忙にもかかわらず快くインタビューに応じていただき，また図版の転載を許可していただいたことを誌上をかりて御礼申しあげます．

The well-known architect of Brazilia's monumental architecture, Oscar Niemeyer, is a central figure in Brazil's modern architecture. Though he has reached the age of 73, he continues his active routine and his works are built all over the world.

Niemeyer's work often employs curves and may be described as sensual. He treats architecture as art, and his work reflects a Brazilian feeling about architecture.

We are here introducing with his own sketches Niemeyer's work of the 70's.

Sketches are not usually used for final presentations, but this method is most appropriate for the expression of Niemeyer's work. This use of the sketch is one of the many things to be learned from Niemeyer.

The sketches shown here were provided by *Modulo, Revista de Arquitetura, Arte e Cultura,* a magazine edited by Niemeyer himself.

We would like to take this opportunity to thank Mr. Niemeyer for interrupting a busy schedule to willingly grant us an interview and for permitting reproduction of these drawings.

ブラジリア大聖堂　CATHEDRAL OF BRASILIA, 1970

この大聖堂の基本的コンセプトは，宗教心を表わすモニュメンタルな造形と，カーブを描く柱が示す祈願と天地の結合である．
The basic concept of this Cathedral is a monumental sculpture with a religious spirit, a gesture of supplication and communication suggested by the curved colums.

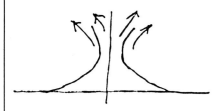

華奢であると同時に官能的な構造は，見るものの空想をさそう．
Delicate and sensuous concrete columns suggest the fantasic.

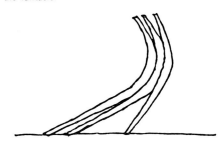

光と影の対比は常に表われる．
The contrast of light and shadow is a constant.

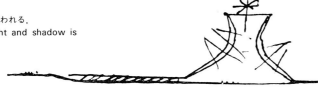

閉鎖的なアプローチは，突然，大聖堂の光と色に満ちた空間で「爆発」し，見るものに，空間の大きな広がりを見せつける．
A narrow and dark approach corridor explose in the main nave, a space with intense color and light, giving to the visitor through the contrast, an impression of a great amplitude.

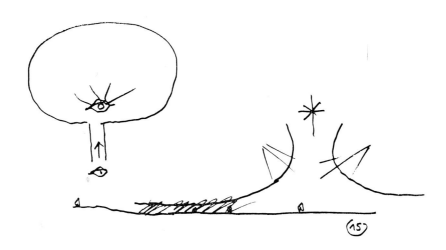

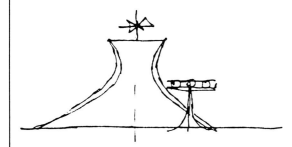

洗礼場をとり囲む空間は，建物の造形に調和するよう工夫が施された．
The baptistery and related spaces are intensively studied to reinforce and harmonize with the structure.

地表に「生じる」身廊部は，閉鎖的な通路を経てきた信者たちの心に，これから始まる宗教儀式への歓びと希望をみなぎらせる．
The cathedral nave sprouting on the surface, lends an atmosphere of pleasure and hope in contrast with the dark approach gallery, preparing the devotees for a religious spectacle.

人類学博物館　MUSEUM OF MAN 1977

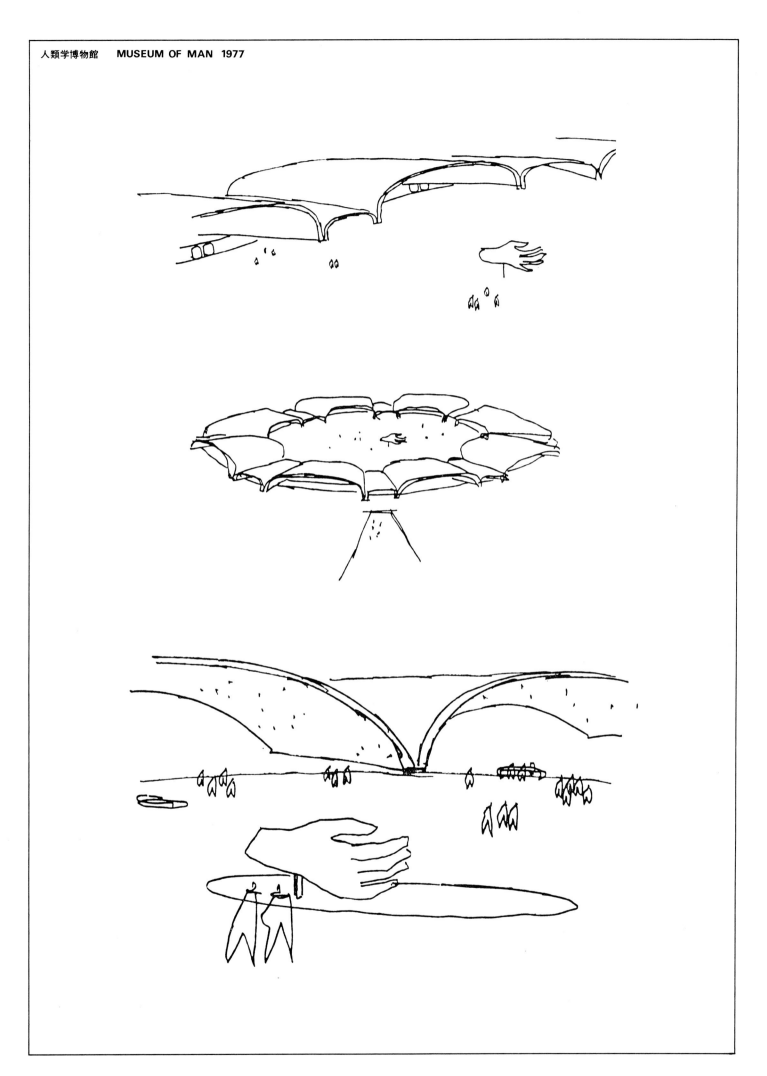

| 人類学博物館　MUSEUM OF MAN 1977 | モンダドリ出版社　MONDADORI, Milano 1968-75 |

狭い通路が,
A dark gallery having openings for the projections of diapositives,

大きな屋内の通りへと続く.
Is connected to a large internal path.

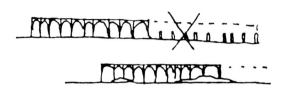

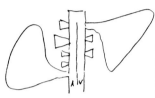

各部分の必要に合わせて,空間を分割し,変化をもたせる.
Divisible and variable spaces were created, according to the problems to each sector.

この場合の構造システムからいえることは,オープン・プランを採用して,グランド・レベルを開放することだ.
The proposed structural system permits the open plan space, liberating the ground level.

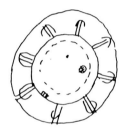

博物館自体は,直径150mの円形をなす.
The museum itself is a circular construction, 150m in diameter.

内側の順路に加えて,突き出た別室も利用できる.
Internal circulation with its auxiliary rooms for projection and exhibits.

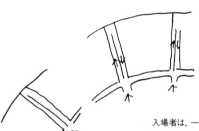

入場者は,一ヶ所だけ見てまわることもできる.
The circulation diagram allows visitors to go through only one sector at a time.

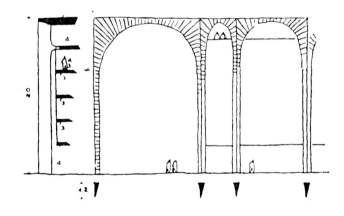

天井の高さと付属室が決められた.
Ceiling heights and annex rooms are defined.

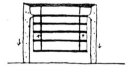

アーチのバリエーションによって,構造上の問題が解決される.
The archs with their varied rythm has no structural problems to be solved.

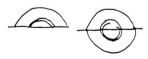

階数の違いは,傾斜地形をうまく生かしている.
Stories vary with the slope, showing the terrain to better advanta.

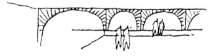

地形が傾斜しているので,閉じた円に主入口を設けることができた.
The slope of the site creates the main entrance and enforces the closed circulation.

16

17

J.J.邸　J.J. HOUSE, Rio de Janeiro 1975

立体による演技と、空間による間とを、うまく演出したい、
A play of volumes and free spaces was sought,

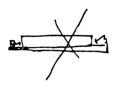

地形のすばらしさを損なうことなしに．
instead of a construction de-emphasizing.

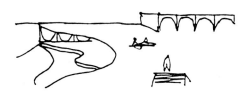

一階は、居間、ホール、書斎とし、庭で囲む．
The living room, hall and study-library are on the ground level, surrounded by generous gardens.

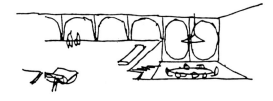

食堂は下の階に置き、台所に直接続ける．
The dining room is located downstairs, directly connected to the kitchen, and

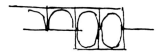

突き出た開口部を通って居間へ．
accessible to the living room through the projected openings.

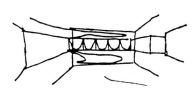

寝室まわりと、大きな居間、そしてレクリエーション室は、同じ階に収める．
On the same level are located the service sector the bedrooms, the large living room and the recreational space.

家は、小さな空間に分けて敷地に合わせるのではなく，
The house is integrated with the site without breaking up into small spaces.

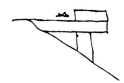

こうするのが、純正な住居には、一番合ったやり方だろう．
It is a simple and radical solution for a pure and classic residence.

バーラ・ダ・チジュッカ計画案

エレベータの数が適切でないと、小さなホールにはいつも混乱が起きるし、緊急の場合は特に危険である．
Confusion is usually the result with several and numerous elevators in a small hall, especially in an emergency.

これを解消するためにニーマイヤーは、コルビュジエの考えを継承して、屋外エレベータと屋外斜路を提唱する．
To solve the problem, Niemeyer, succeeding le Corbusier's plan, suggests an exterior location for elevators and ramps.

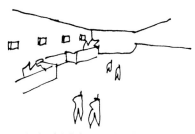

エレベータから出ると、広い通りと快適な庭がひろがる．これはまた、居住者のプライヴァシーを守るとともに、緊急時の問題も解消してくれる．
The elevators open to a wide comfortable street and gardens. This both protects residential privacy and solves problems of movement in cases of emergency.

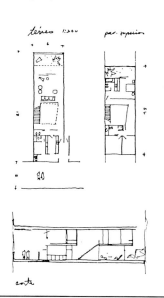

TWO PROJECTS FOR BARRA DA TIJUCA, 1977

イーリャ・プーラ　Ilha Pura

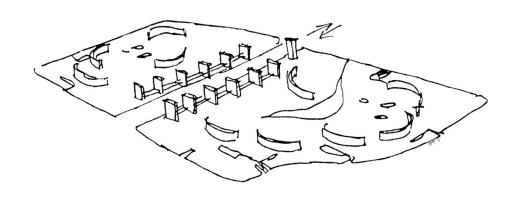

クリシーカ　Curicica

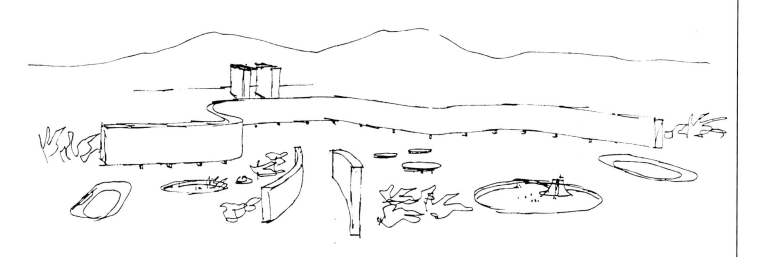

敷地と街路とのレベル差は，駐車場，学校など，様々な用途に活用される．
The difference in level between the terrain and the street can be used for many purposes, such as parking space, schools, etc.

Illustrations from "MÓDULO": Revista de Arquitetura, Arte e Cultura. Compilation and Commentary by H.Yamaki, based on the existing text.

CARVALHAL RESIDENCE
Ponta do Parurú, Ibiúna, São Paulo, 1977
Architect: Decio Tozzi

カルバリアウ邸
サンパウロ州イビウーナ市ポンタ・ド・パルルー
設計：デーシオ・トッズィ

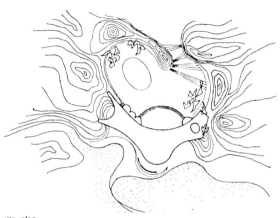

site plan

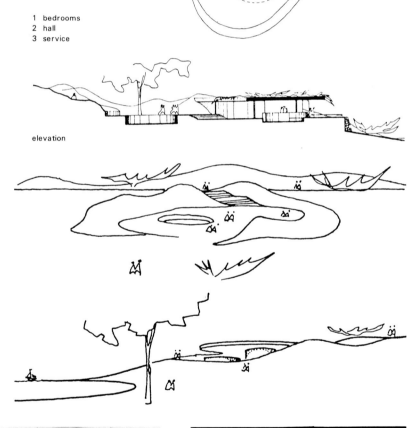

plan

1 bedrooms
2 hall
3 service

elevation

この週末住居のうねるような外形は，周囲にある川岸とそのまわりを取り巻く丘の描く曲線から発想されたものである．プランは充分なプライバシーを保障し，大きく広々とした中庭を取り囲むように構成されている．

庭園にとけ込んだ屋根が各部屋をおおい，サービス関係の諸施設は組積造の壁で囲まれている．そしてリビング・エリアは内部と外部の景色を連続的に結びつけるように，透明なガラスで仕切られた中に置かれている．

オスカー・ニーマイヤーはこの住宅について次のように述べている．「カルバリアウ邸においては，斜面や高低差のある地形にみごとに溶け込んだ伸びのある形態が目を引く」．

The rolling outline of this weekend home is suggested by the curving lines of the river bank and the surrounding hills. The plan itself is organized around a large and generous courtyard, affording necessary privacy.

A gardened roof shelters the rooms and services enclosed by masonry; the living area is located in a transparent frame, making a continuous space connecting the exterior scenery and the interior.

Oscar Niemeyer says of this house: "In the Carvalhal residence the free form dominates, gracefully accompanying the topography in its slopings and levels."

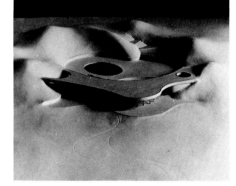

ABREU RESIDENCE
Fazenda Veneza, Valinhos, São Paulo, 1976
Architect : Decio Tozzi

アブレウ邸
サンパウロ州バリンニョス市ファゼンダ・ベネーザ
設計:デーシオ・トッズィ

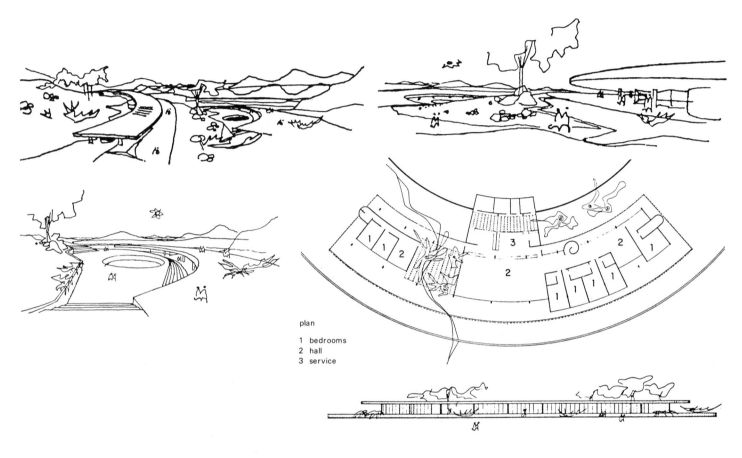

plan
1 bedrooms
2 hall
3 service

elevation

この建築は，土地の形態から創られている．そのデザインは周囲の景色を変更せずに敷地の曲線を生かすことによって生み出されている．そこには，向かいあって大きな弧を描く形態の対話がある．ここでは建築技術がその環境とのやりとりの中で考えられているのである．

変化に富んだ内容が，いくつかの解放的な生活空間を内包する一つの単純な形の中に納められており，その形はファゼンダ・ベネーザ渓谷の曲りくねった流れの動きに呼応している．

This architecture rises from the landscape, its design suggested by the curves of the site, leaving the surrounding scenery unaltered; a dialogue of large curved gestures is established. Building technique is here caught in an exchange with its surroundings.

The diversified program is sheltered under a single element with open living spaces, echoing the movement of the curves of Fazenda Veneza valley.

ITORORÓ VILLAGE URBAN RENOVATION
Bela Vista, São Paulo, 1976
Architect : Decio Tozzi

イトロロー再開発
サンパウロ市ベーラ・ビスタ
設計：デーシオ・トッズィ

この一画は，もともとイトロロー・バレーという場所に1940年代に建築された37軒の家が集まっていた．折衷主義の色あいが濃いこれらの建物からは，ポルトガルから移民してきたフランシスコ・デ・カストロという人の非凡な想像力が感じられる．

敷地はサンパウロの谷になっている場所でよく見られるようにかなり不整形である．中心を通る折れ曲った軸によってこの一画では有機的なつながりが生みだされており，特に広場はポルトガルや地中海の集落にみられるものよりもはるかにそのあたりの空間を豊かなものにしている．工事にあたっては，街区全体に対し記念碑的な性格を付与し，一つのまとまった集合体を創り出すために，以前に使用されていた材料を混ぜ合せて用いている．

この改造によって，街は文化的なアイデンティティを獲得するとともに，サンパウロにおける建築の歴史を人々が理解するための一助となるという役割を担っている．この計画に続く次の段階として，都市改造の理念に合致した種々の技法を用いる計画が予定されている．

The Village was originally a group of 37 houses constructed during the 1940's in the Itororó Valley. Characterized by electicism, these houses reflect the uncommon imagination of Francisco de Castro, a Portugese immigrant.

The site has a very irregular topography characteristic of São Paulo's valleys. A central winding axis organizes the Village; piazzetas enrich the space much as in Portugese and Mediterranean villages. The construction incorporates salvaged materials in the design, lending a degree of monumentality to the whole and creating a singular grouping.

It is hoped the renovation will give the complex a cultural identity and help preserve the elements by which we may understand the history of São Paulo's architecture. The project continues in stages using techniques consistent with ideals of renovation.

stege 1

stege 2

stege 3

27

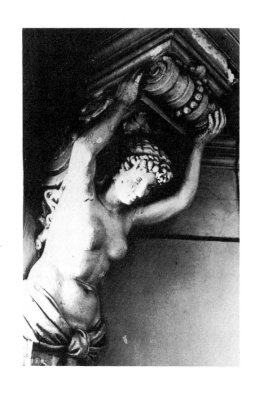

CAMPOS DO JORDÃO TELEPHONE EXCHANGE

Abernéssia, Campos do Jordão, São Pauio, 1973
Architect: Ruy Ohtake

カンポス・ド・ジョルドン電話交換局

サンパウロ州カンポス・ド・ジョルドン

設計：ルイ・オータケ

カンポス・ド・ジョルドンの市街はサンパウロの北東190kmにあるマンチケーラ山の麓に位置する気候の温暖な避暑地である．電話局はアベルネッシア・スタチオン公園の一隅に位置し，広場の延長として計画された．

　プレストレスト・コンクリートを主構造としており，18mにおよぶはね出しが2本の柱で支えられている．電話交換室と公衆便所が上の階におかれ，他の施設はすべて下の階に収められている．

　最初に計画された広場に合わせて，建物の構造は，敷地の中でランドマークとなりうる力強い造形表現を持つように設計されている．

The city of Campos do Jordão is a warm-weather resort located on Mantiquera mountain, 190 km northeast of São Paulo. The telephone exchange is located at one side of the Abernéssia Station garden. The project was conceived as an extension of the plaza.

The structure is of prestressed concrete; the 18-meter overhang is suported by two columns. The telephone cabine and public toilets are located on the upper level and all facilities on the lower.

In accord with the initial proposal, the structural solution has a vigorous plastic expression, serving as a landmark on the site.

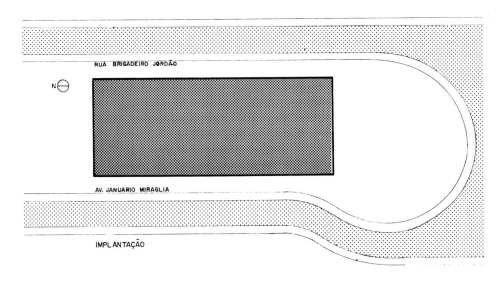

site plan

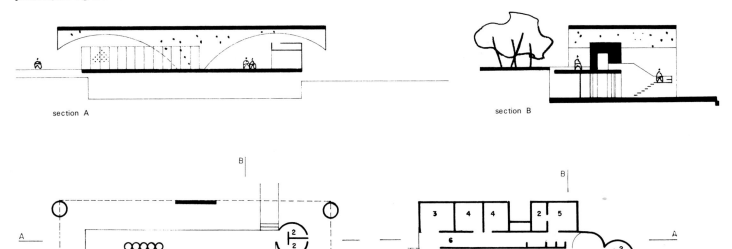

section A

section B

upper floor

lower floor

1 cabin
2 WC
3 air conditioning
4 storage
5 storehouse
6 archive
7 offices

IBIÚNA TELEPHONE EXCHANGE
Ibiúna, São Paulo, 1974
Architect: Ruy Ohtake

イビウーナ電話交換局

サンパウロ州イビウーナ

設計：ルイ・オータケ

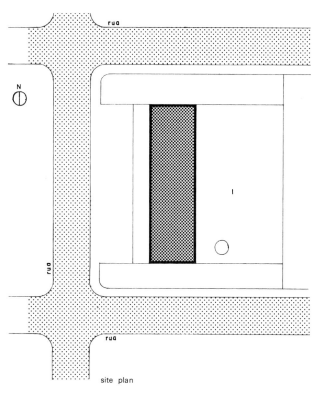

site plan

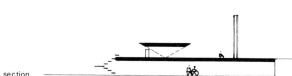

section

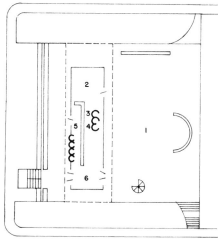

upper floor

lower floor

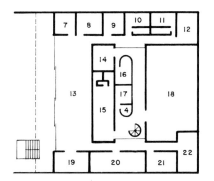

1 plaza
2 administration
3 pantry
4 WC
5 service station
6 waiting room
7 meters
8 transformers
9 generator
10 adjusters
11 batteries
12 air conditioning
13 garage
14 trnsmission
15 commutation
16 transmission workshop
17 commutation workshop
18 local commutation
19 storehouse
20 workshop
21 WC and cloakroom
22 general distributor

この建物の敷地は主として三つの面から成り，高低差が5mもある斜面となっている．計画された建物はこの敷地の特徴を生かし，広場を創り出している．

すべての設備は下の階におさめられ，広場に面した一角には一般の人々が使用する軽々とした形態の空間が置かれている．でき上がった空間は視覚的には広々とした感じを残しながら最大限有効に利用されている．

The site on which this building is located has three faces and an accentuated slope of five meters. The solution exploits this characteristic and creates a plaza.

All equipment is located on the lower level and a light plastic volume for public use occupies one corner of the plaza. The resulting space is maximized while remaining visually open.

33

BANESPA BUTANTÃ BANK

Butantã, São Paulo, 1976
Architect : Ruy Ohtake

バネスパ・ブタンタン銀行
サンパウロ市ブタンタン
設計：ルイ・オータケ

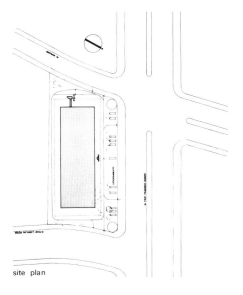

site plan

1 expedient
2 cashier
3 manager
4 cabin
5 air conditioning
6 pantry
7 WC for women
8 WC for men
9 filing
10 storehouse
11 safebox
12 strongbox

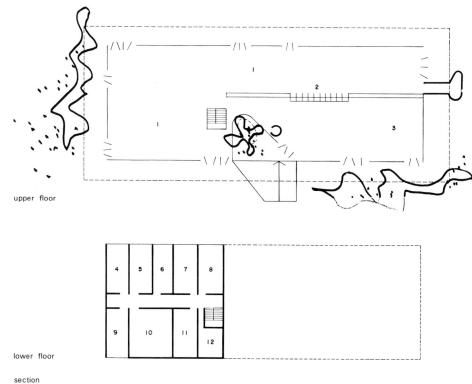

upper floor

lower floor

section

この支店は市の中心部への主要な道であるフランシスコ・モラット通りに位置している．このような街路では，様々な様式と形態を持つ建物の建ち並ぶ種々雑多な景観が特長である．

このように錯綜した都市景観の中にあって，この建物には非常に軽快な造形的表現が与えられている．構造は4本の柱状の部分に支えられたプレストレスト・コンクリートから成る．内部は二つのレベルに分かれ，地上レベルは一般の人々の利用に供され，下のレベルは管理部門となっている．

This branch is located on Francisco Morato Avenue, a major approach to the city. Such corridors are usually characterized by a heterogeneous scenery consisting of various building types and forms.

Sited within such complex urban scenery, this building has a very light plstic design. The structure is of prestressed concrete supported by four columns. Divided into two levels, the ground level is for public use and the lower level for administration.

35

CETESB LABORATORY
São Paulo, 1976
Architect: Ruy Ohtake

セテスビ研究所

サンパウロ市

設計：ルイ・オータケ

遠隔計測工学研究所のためのこの計画においてそこに表現された美学と空間の流動性は容易に見てとれる．

トイレを内蔵する拡大された構造壁とコンピューター室のためのシリンダーがこの空間を限定し，補強している．地下はユーティリティと倉庫を収容するようデザインされている．

室内温度を快適に保つため特別のディテールが採用された．屋根の上にある鏡状の水面が太陽光の与える影響を調節し，必要に応じて室内空間を保護しているのである．

Aesthetics and fluidity of space are evident in this project for a telemetrical laboratory.

Enlarged structural walls containing the toilets and a cylinder for the computer room define and reinforce the space. The basement is designed to house utilities and storage.

Special details were used to enhance thermal comfort. A water mirror on the roof attenuates effects of the sun and gives necessary protection to the sheltered space.

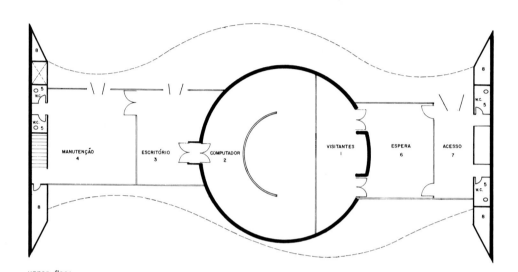
upper floor

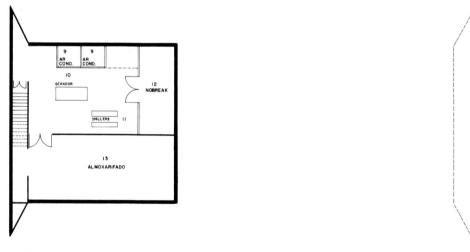
lower floor

1 visitors
2 computers
3 office room
4 maintenance room
5 WC
6 waiting room
7 access
8 piping
9 air conditioning
10 generator
11 shillers
12 nobreak
13 storehouse

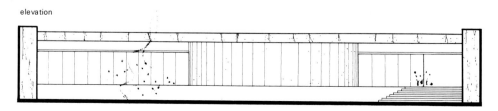
elevation

ÁGUAS DA PRATA BALNEARY

Aguas da Prata, São Paulo, 1974
Architect: João Walter Toscano

アーグアス・ダ・プラタ保養所
サンパウロ州アーグアス・ダ・プラタ市
設計：ジョアオ・ヴァウテル・トスカーノ

アーグアス・ダ・プラタはサンパウロの北200kmのところに位置し，大へん豊かな自然景観に恵まれた温泉地である．この計画では，解放的な質を有しながらかつ地方的な景観と建築の各部分が，統一感のある敷地利用のモデルを創り出すことが意図されている．

この工事でもっとも特徴的なことは，国の保護林に隣接する敷地そのものを尊重したことであり，集会や文化活動，スポーツの諸施設それぞれへのアプローチを大切にしたことである．浴室のための諸施設，集会室，展示ホール，劇場等がプログラムの中に盛り込まれている．

中心となる建物と劇場のボリュームは，簡潔なまとまりをもって敷地の中に配置されている．階別に諸機能が振り分けられ，上層階はパンチングメタルでできた半透過性のブリーズ・ソレイユを用いることによって外の景色を楽しめるように工夫された浴室があり，中間階は集会やレクリエーションのための施設が配置され，そこはいわば街路のような役割を果たしている．そして下の階には，管理部門，医務室，設備関係の諸室などが配置されている．

Aguas da Prata is a bathing resort situated 200 km (120 mile) north of São Paulo, in a landscape of great richness. This project is an attempt to create a model for site utilization, retaining an open quality and integrating architectural elements with the local scenery.

The principal characteristic of the construction is respect for the site itself, being contiguous to a State forest reserve, and a local approach to social, cultural, and sports facilities. Equipped spaces for pools, meeting places, exhibition hall and auditorium, complete the program.

The site is occupied by a compact block composed of two volumes, the main building and the auditorium. Functions are distributed by level. On the upper level are baths made visually open to the scenery by semi-transparent brise-soliel; the intermediate level contains the social and recreation activities and acts as a street; on the lower level are administrative and doctor's offices and supporting facilities.

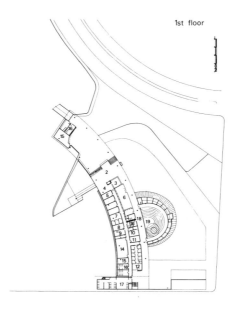

1st floor

1st floor
1. Main Hall
2. Waitingroom
3. Reception
4. Waiting
5. Doctor's office
6. Administration
7. Light Applicationroom
8. Laboratory
9. Pharmacy
10. X-Ray
11. Storehouse
12. Waitingroom
13. Bathroom
14. Laundry
15. Storage
16. WC
17. Cloackroom for the Pool
18. Corridor
19. Auditorium

2nd floor
1. Pool
2. Children's pool
3. Pump
4. Cloackroom
5. Machineroom
6. Shop
7. WC
8. Cafeteria
9. Livingroom
10. Terrace
11. Large Hall
12. Slope

3rd floor
1. Hall
2. Control
3. Clerk Room
4. Doctor
5. Cloackroom/WC
6. Inhalation, Pulverization
7. Barder
8. Coiffeur
9. Gimnastic
10. Bathroom
11. Sauna
12. Vapor
13. Douche
14. Pool
15. Scotch Douche
16. Massage
17. Restroom
18. Bar

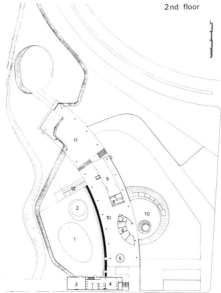

2nd floor

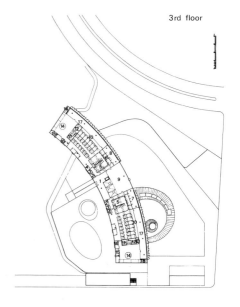

3rd floor

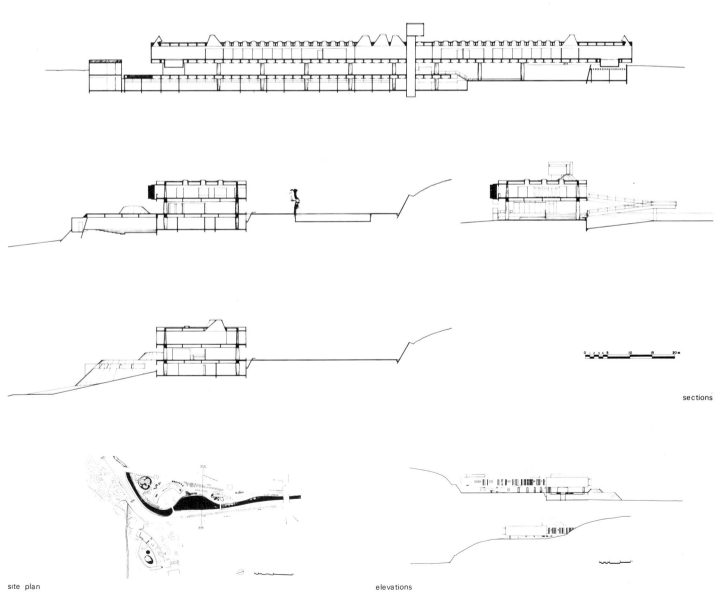

sections

site plan	elevations

ARARAQUARA UNIVERSITY CAMPUS

Araraquara, São Paulo, 1974
Architect : João Walter Toscano

アララクァーラ大学
サンパウロ州アララクァーラ市
設計：ジョアオ・ヴァウテル・トスカーノ

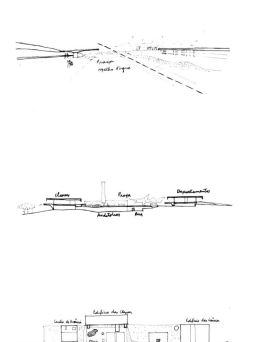

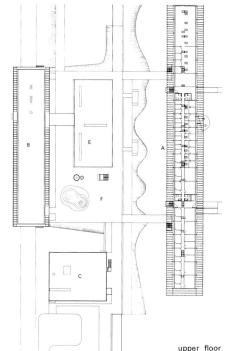

Upper floor

A. BLOCK OF DEPARTMENTS
   UPPER FLOOR
B. BLOCK OF CLASSROOMS
C. SOCIAL CENTER
D. WATER RESERVOIR
E. WATER MIRROR
F. PLAZA

Ground floor

A. BLOCK OF DEPATMENTS
   GROUND FLOOR
B. BLOCK OF CLASSROOMS
   UPPER FLOOR
C. SOCIAL CENTER
   GROUND FLOOR
D. WATER RESERVOIR
E. WATER MIRROR
F. PLAZA

Ground & Basement floor

A. BLOCK OF DEPARTMENT
B. BLOCK OF CLASSROOMS
C. SOCIAL CENTRE
   LOWER FLOOR

upper floor

このキャンパスは次の3つの条件，すなわち(1)学科の増設，(2)教育機構の変更，(3)様々な交流活動，に対応できるよう計画されている．

　この目的を達成するために二つの重要な要素が導入された．一つは敷地のレベル差をぬって交流のための場所とオーディトリアムおよび展示のための場所を結びつけている縦方向の軸であり，もう一つは建物群をまとめている広場である．これらの二つの要素はおおいのある歩行空間およびスロープとしてキャンパス全体の動線を形づくっている．

This campus is designed to allow for (1) an increased faculty; (2) changes in the teaching structure; and (3) a variety of social activities.

This objective accordingly developed two principal elements — a longitudinal axis organizing the site levels and connecting the social areas, the auditorium, and the exhibition areas; and a plaza orienting the buildings. These two elements establish the movement of the complex by means of covered walks and slopes.

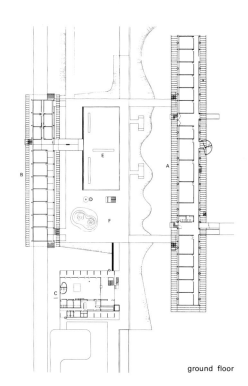

ground floor

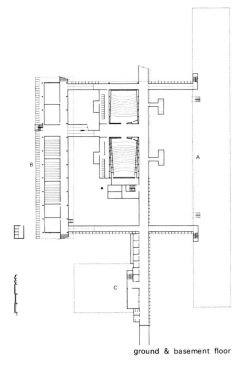

ground & basement floor

44

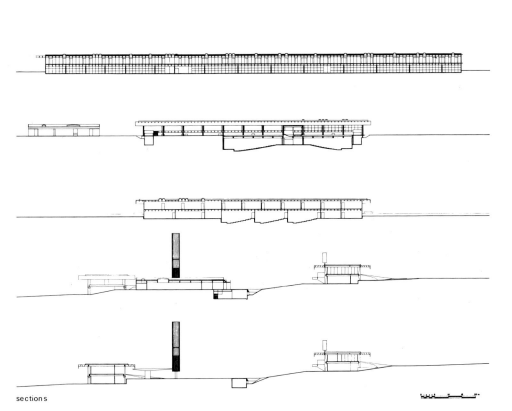
sections

JÚLIO DE MESQUITA FILHO HOSPITAL

Marginal do Tietê, São Paulo, 1974
Architect: Fabio Penteado & Teru Tamaki

ジューリオ・デ・メスキータ・フィリオ病院

サンパウロ市マルジナール・ド・チエテー

設計:F・ペンテアド,T・タマキ

サンタ・カーザ病院は1607年に設立されたサンパウロ市で一番古い病院である．1971年に市当局から寄付された土地を加えて病院側がすでに購入していた土地に，新たにサンタ・カーザ財団の既存の施設を増築することになっている．チエテー河畔にあるこの敷地は全体で240,000m²にのぼり，新しくできる病院と附属の学校の特色ともなるだろう．

ここには，教育・保健・レジャー施設を統合したものが予定されている．この計画の基本的な特徴を次にあげると，(1)医療と教育分野の統合，(2)多様な機能的要求への対応，(3)医療の専門家を養成する学校の設備さらに，(4)機能的な要求のみならず人間的な尺度と美しさによって特徴づけられる空間のデザイン，である．

この基本的な考え方を尊重して，建物は1街区にわたる3層の低いデザインになった．広い中央広場は通行の要であるとともにすべての内部空間を体系づけている．この広場は広い庭と自然光を特色とし，楽しげな健康的な雰囲気を作り出すように計画されている．

広場に面した空間にはそれぞれ別の機能，すなわち病院，医学校，購売部，救急病棟が設けられる．

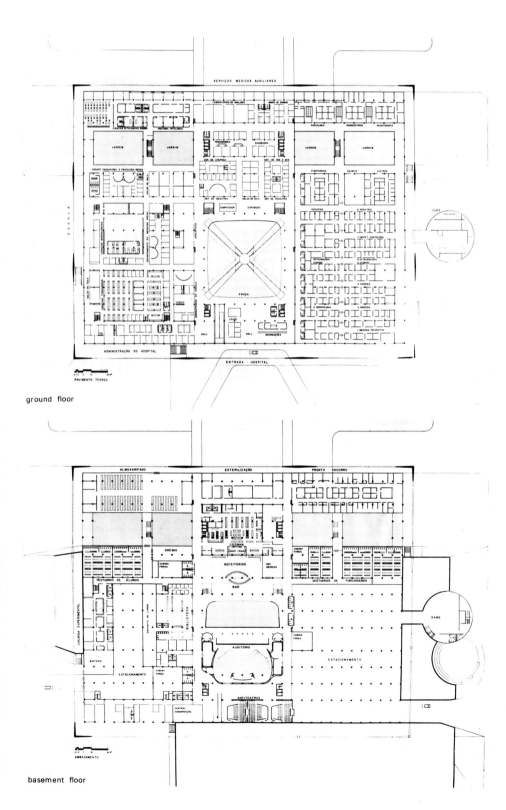

ground floor

basement floor

The Santa Casa Hospital, established in 1607, was the first hospital in the city of São Paulo. The existing facilities of the Santa Casa Foundation will be expanded to a new site donated by the municipal government in 1971 and adjoining land bought by the Foundation. The site, with a total area of 240,000 m² situated on the bank of the Tietê River, will feature a new hospital and annexed school.

The complex will integrate education, health, and leisure facilities. The basic features of this project are: (1) its integration of medical and education circles; (2) its response to diverse functional requirements; (3) the provision of a school for medical technicians; and (4) the design of spaces characterized not only by functional necessities but a sensitivity to human scale and aesthetics.

Respect for the initial concepts led to a low-rise design with only three stories covering a single block. A large central plaza becomes a traffic node and unifies all internal spaces. The plaza, featuring extensive landscaping and natural light, is intended to create an atmosphere of optimism and health.

Each face of the plaza assumes a distinctive function: hospital, medical school, supporting facilities and first aid clinic.

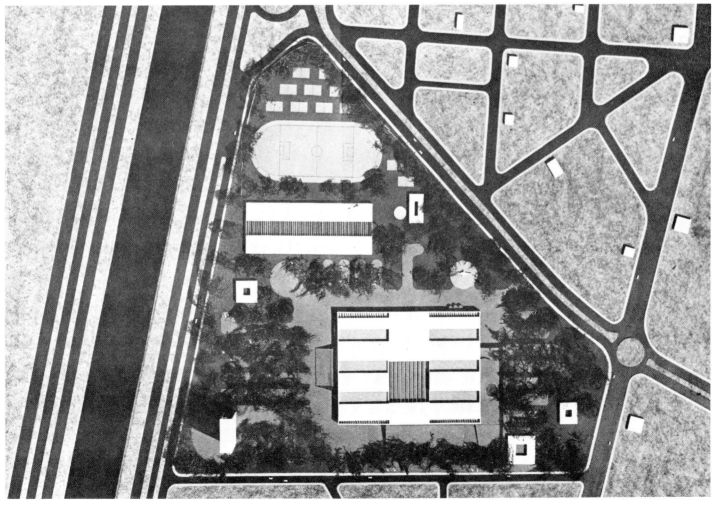

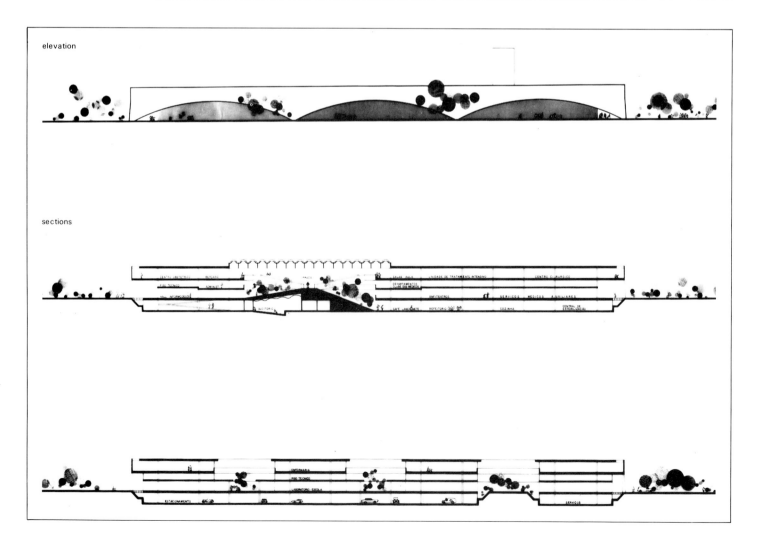

elevation

sections

CALUX KINDERGARTEN

Sao Bernardo do Campo, São Paulo, 1978
Architect: Paulo Mendes da Rocha

カルックス幼稚園
サンパウロ州サン・ベルナルド・ド・カンポ
設計：パウロ・メンデス・ダ・ローシャ

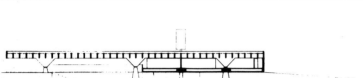
section

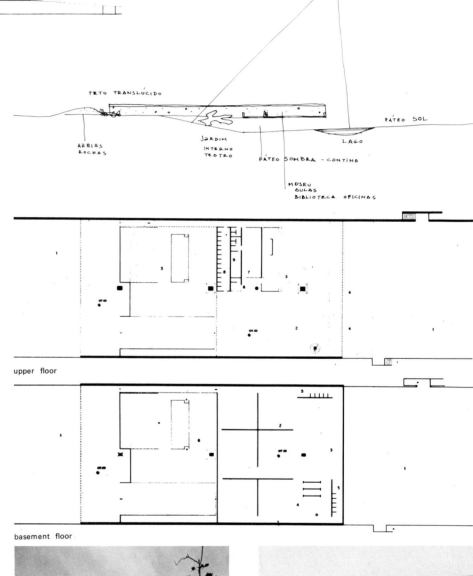
upper floor

basement floor

この計画を進めていく中で，計画チームはいくつかの問題点をひろい出した．それによると，近年，文字通り子供の園としての幼稚園についての考え方が変わってきており，教室を廊下でつなぐ方式は妥当な解法とはいえず，庭の中に配した教室群を舗装した小径でつなぐ方法をとることになった．

幼稚園には自然に対する好奇心や環境を学んでゆく機会がたくさんなければならない．この計画では，幼児にふさわしいと思われているものの，ばかげた模造品にすぎないものを造るのではなく，自然，大地，水，宇宙，生命を示すことに力点がおかれている．

砂と小石で舗装され水の流れている小路によって，周囲の空間は建物の中へ導かれ，この小径全体を覆ってすべての施設を内包する 800㎡ の建物が置かれている．また内外のつなぎの空間には木を形どった支柱が設けられている．実施案は，特殊な納まりは用いずに，ごく普通の鉄筋コンクリート造で，単純明快な表情を持っている．

The design team for this project took a new look at some accepted notions. The idea of the kindergarten, literally "child garden", has been changed in some recent projects by construction of classrooms with corridors, considered inadequate solutions to the problem by these planners, and with paved paths substituted for the garden.

The designers felt the kindergarten must be a place where the learning process is encouraged, relating the environment to natural curiosity about nature. By presenting nature, soil, water, the cosmos, all of life, as facts, the project avoids the pitfall of imitation, a method which the planners considered detrimental.

The surrounding space enters the building as a continuous path with sand, gravel and water. Above this path is located an 800 square meter space containing all facilities. The transitional space between the interior and exterior is similar to the overspreading branches of a tree.

The proposed solution is extremely simple, consisting of a reinforced concrete structure without refined details.

CECAP TAUBATÉ HOUSING DEVELOPMENT
Quiririm, Taubaté, São Paulo, 1973
Architect: Bonilha & Sancovski

セカッピ・タウバテー・ハウジング
サンパウロ州タウバテー市キリリン
設計：ボニーリャ＆サンコーヴィスキー

この計画案が実施される敷地は「丘の海」と呼ばれているこの地方特有の地形を呈し，全域で628ヘクタールある．

十分な検討を経た試案によれば，最終段階において，住戸数2770，推定人口13,850,850人，ヘクタール当り220人の人口密度になる．

こういう地形と，敷地の一部分を分断するように通過しているハイウェイによって基本的方針が決まった．CECAPによって確立された前提条件に沿って話を進めると，住区は住戸と少数のアパートから成っている．主なアパート群と商店街はハイウェイのそばに位置している．

典型的な複合体は「村」であり80m四方の区画に，造園された広場を中心として約40戸の家がひとかたまりとなっている．家々はこの広場の周囲に配置されることにより，内部にコミニュティ広場として使われる私的な空間をつくりだしている．

各々の「村」には主な進入路が一つと1，2ヶ所の近隣との通路が用意されている．道路を意図的に曲げることにより，主に歩行者のためのモールを創り出そうとしている．

The site on which this project is constructed has a total area of 628 hectares, with typical local topography characterized by a "sea of hills."

The elaborated pilot plan has 2770 residential units supporting a probable population of 13,850 inhabitants with a density of 220 persons per hectare in the final stage. The general concept is determined by the topography and a crossing highway, dividing a part of the area.

To proceed by the premis established by CECAP, the residential zone consists of house units and a fewer number of apartments. The main group of apartments and the commercial zone were located near the highway.

The typical grouping of the complex is the "villa", or group of approximately 40 houses in landscaped squares of 80 × 80 meters. The houses are organized around the perimeter of the square, creating an inner private space to be used as a community plaza. Each villa has a main access and one or two secondary accesses to neighboring plazas. The intentional sinuousity of circulation is intended to create a mall mainly for pedestrians.

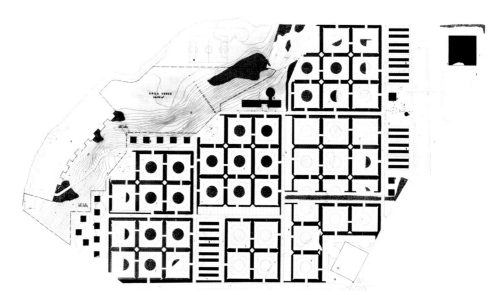
site plan

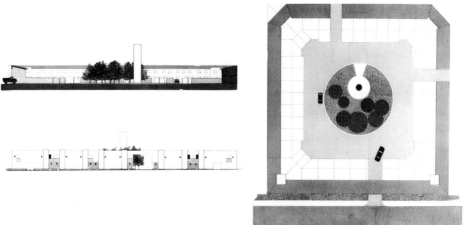
house units: plan and elevation

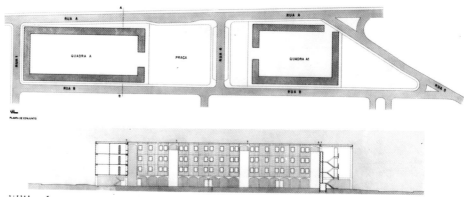
apartment: plan and elevation

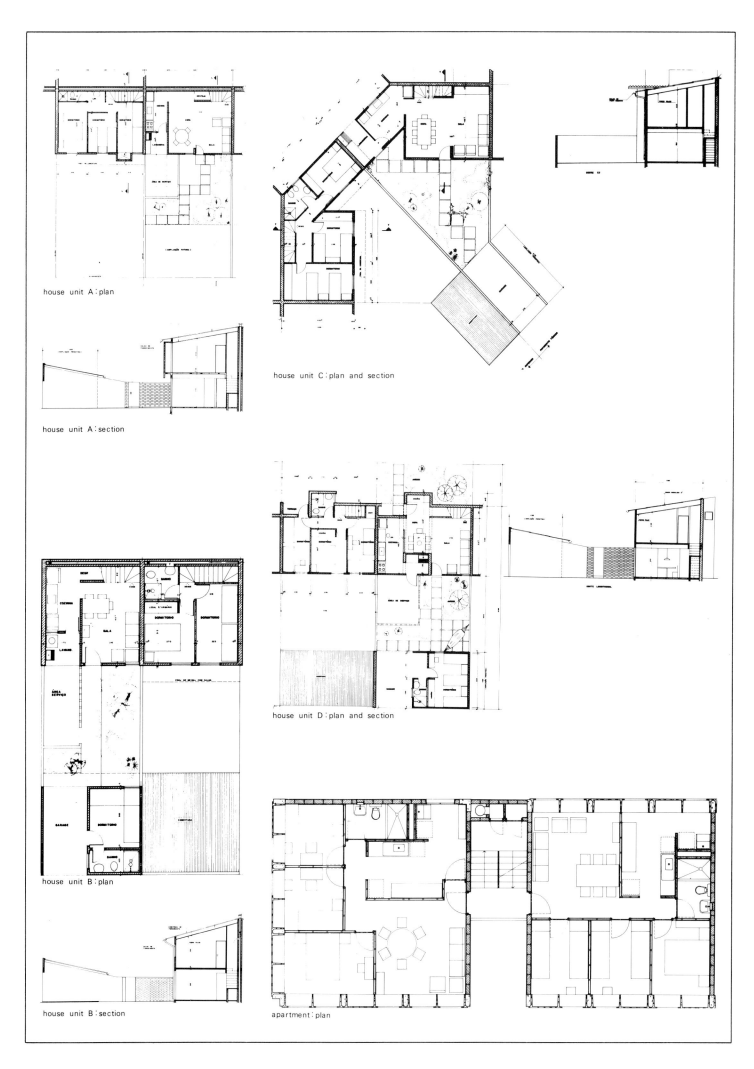

MORUMBI OFFICE BUILDING
R. George Eastman, Morumbi, São Paulo, 1972
Architect : Bonilha & Sancovski

モルンビー・オフィス・ビルディング
サンパウロ市モルンビー区ジェオルジェ・イースチマン
設計：ボニーリャ＆サンコーヴィスキー

この計画は長年にわたって共に働いてきた建築家とエンジニアたちのグループの間で生まれた．この建物はグループの本部であり，建築計画のあらゆる段階において効率的な仕事ができるよう計画された．このグループがまず建物のデザインに関心を持った時，達成すべき目標は質のよい建築をローコストでいかに実現するかということであった．ピロティとエレベータ・シャフトが地盤面から立ち上がっているだけで，急勾配の敷地にもかかわらず土工事はほとんど行わなかった．

気候にあわせ，外壁には開口部がない．テラスは自然採光に役立つとともに直射日光がさしこまないように内部空間を保護している．

十分に断熱をほどこしたプレファブ化されたコンクリートパネルとブロックが内部空間を生み出すために用いられた．

この計画の中ではオフィス空間の他に，食堂，居間的な空間，コピールーム，電話交換室，管理人室等の共有施設を最上階や低層部に設けた．

This enterprise grew from a group of architects and engineers who had been working together for a long time. It was intended to be the headquarters of the group, a place where they could work efficiently on all phases of an architectural project.

As the group is primarily concerned with building design, the challenge was to realize good architecture at low cost. No excavation was needed on the steep site; the pilotis and elevator shaft rise from the ground.

Appropriate to the climate, exterior walls are blank; terraces allow for natural lighting and protection from the sun for the internal spaces.

Insulated wall consisting of prefabricated concrete panels and blocks were employed for closed areas. Besides an office area, the project provides common use facilities such as lunchroom, living, copyroom, telephone exchange, caretaker's room, etc., on the penthouse and lower levels.

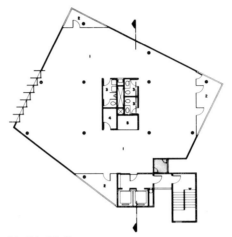

6th, 7th, 8th floor

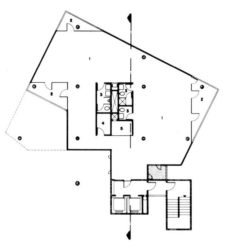

1st floor

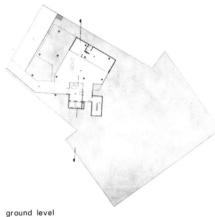

ground level

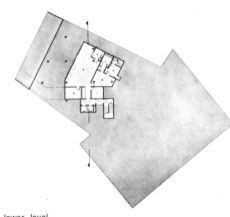

lower level

6th, 7th, 8th floor
1 offices
2 terraces
3 WC
4 pantry
5 air conditioner

1st floor
1 offices
2 terraces
3 WC
4 pantry
5 air conditioner

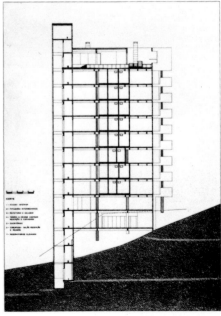

section

J. O. MAIA RESIDENCE
R. Albert Einstein, Morumbi, São Paulo, 1973
Architect : Bonilha & Sancovski

J・O・マイア邸

サンパウロ州モルンビー市アウベルチ・アインステイン

設計：ボニーリャ＆サンコーヴィスキー

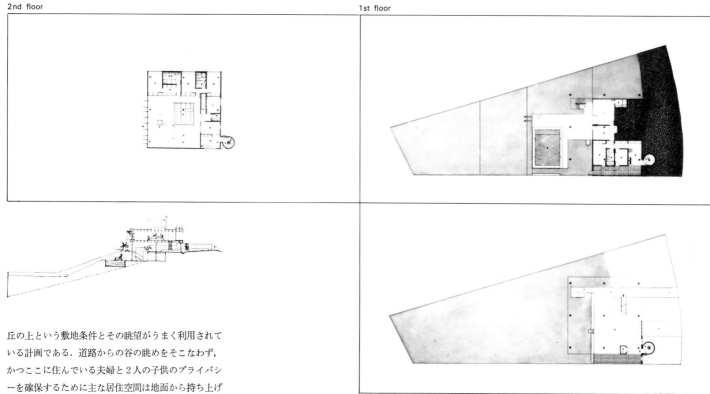

丘の上という敷地条件とその眺望がうまく利用されている計画である．道路からの谷の眺めをそこなわず，かつここに住んでいる夫婦と2人の子供のプライバシーを確保するために主な居住空間は地面から持ち上げられている．

　その他の生活空間やプールを含むレクリエーションのための施設および機械室は，道路よりも低いところに設けられた．

　主体構造はピロティに支えられた現場打ちコンクリートで外壁は組石造になっている．

　この地方の気候にふさわしい，ブリーズ・ソレイユはプレキャストコンクリート造である．

　広大なまわりの景観は必要なプライバシーを守るのに十分でかつ接客空間にはすばらしい雰囲気をつくり出している．

This project takes advantage of its hill-top site and vista. In order to preserve the view of the valley from the street and achieve privacy for the residents, a couple with two children, the main dwelling is raised above the ground. Additional living space, recreational facilities including a pool, and mechanical systems are located below the street level.

　The main structure is of poured-in-place reinforced conrete on pilotis with external walls of masonry. The brise-soleil, appropriate to the local climate, is of prefabricated concrete. An extensive landscape offers necessary privacy and atmosphere to the social area.

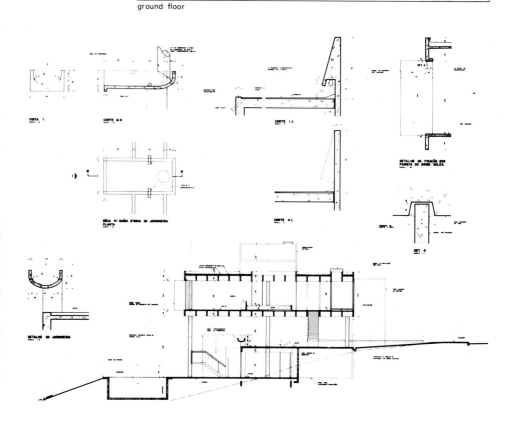

VERONEZZI RESIDENCE
R. Heron Domingues, São Paulo, 1977
Architect : Bonilha & Sancovski

ベロネッズィ邸
サンパウロ市エーロン・ドミンゲス
設計：ボニーリャ＆サンコーヴィスキー

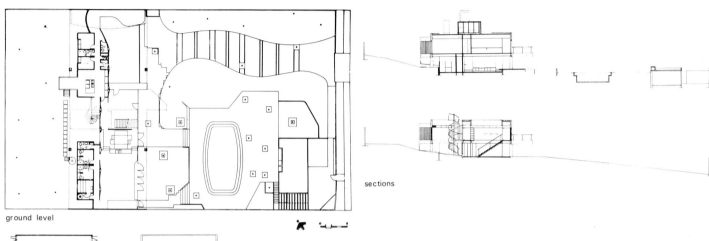

ground level

sections

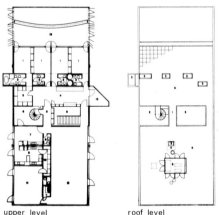

upper level   roof level

この家は夫婦と二人の子供と祖母のために設計されている．ユーカリの木におおわれた傾斜面であることを考慮にいれ，機能を二層に分けて配している．上層は家族の私的な生活の場であり，下層はサウナ室やプールを含む社交的な活動の場となっている．

この家は従来どおりの現場打ちコンクリート造で4本の柱で支えられている．ダクトや空調の設備空間は床スラブと天井との間に設けられている．

This house is designed for a couple with two children and their grandmother. It takes account of the sloping site, covered with Eucalyptus trees, by assigning functions to two levels. The upper level is for the family's private life, while the lower, containing sauna and pool, is for social activities.

The house is a conventional reinforced concrete structure supported by four columns. A mechanical space for ducts and airconditioning is provided between the slab and the ceiling.

63

PIRAQUÊ INDUSTRY

Madureira, Rio de Janeiro, 1977
Architect: Marcello Fragelli

ピラケー・インダストリー
リオデジャネイロ市マドレイラ
設計：マルセーロ・フラジェリ

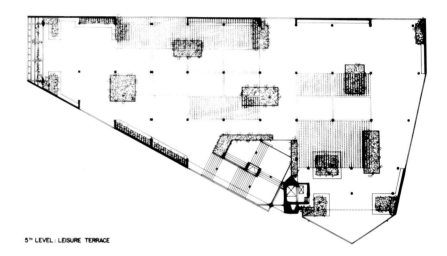

5TH LEVEL: LEISURE TERRACE

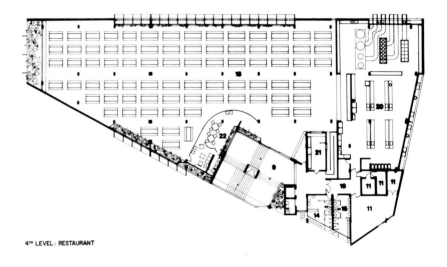

4TH LEVEL: RESTAURANT

この建物はリオデジャネイロの郊外でかなり密度の高い地区にある規模の小さい敷地に立っており，食品加工工場がこの中に収容されている．

建物のプログラムは次のとおりである．地上階には自動車のためのサービス・ステーションがあり，2階には，応接関係の施設と医務室などの職員関係の施設がある．3階にはロッカー室と洗面所，4階には職員休憩室があり，さらにその上のなかば半室内化された屋上庭園のテラスも休息のための場所として計画されている．

自動車のためのサービス・ステーションへは細い道が主要なアクセスとなり，洗車したり注油したりする場所へは表の道からアプローチする．主要な立面には職員用の入口と各階を結ぶ階段室が含まれている．

この外気に面している階段室は，ファサードの視覚的変化の中で力強い部分を構成している．

This building houses a food-processing plant located on a small lot in a high-density suburb of Rio de Janeiro.

The program includes a ground-level service station for the vehicle fleet; social amenities and personnel facilities, such as a medical center, on the second floor; lockers and lavatories on the third; and a canteen on the fourth floor. A semi-enclosed roof-top garden terrace was designed as a leisure area.

Principal access to the vehicle service station is from a minor street while the washing and lubricating cells are reached from a collector road. The main facade contains the personnel entrance and the staircase linking all floors.

The open staircase constitutes a forceful element in the visual dynamics of the facade.

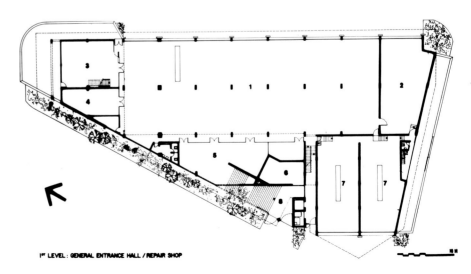

1ST LEVEL: GENERAL ENTRANCE HALL / REPAIR SHOP

65

PONTE PEQUENA METRO STATION

Ponte Pequena, São Paulo, 1973
Architect: Marcello Fragelli

ポンテ・ペケーナ地下鉄駅

サンパウロ市ポンテ・ペケーナ

設計：マルセーロ・フラジェリ

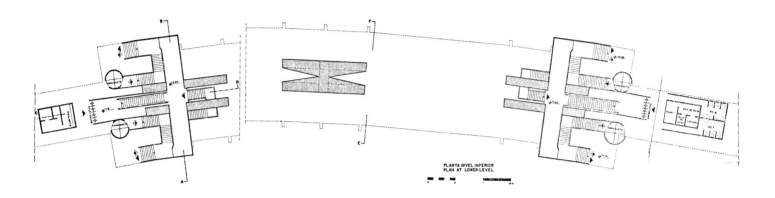

サンパウロ地下鉄は都心部における過去10年間の開発の中でもっとも重要なものである．この計画では本線から横枝のように分かれて地上に現われてくる高架部分を，統一のとれた構造体として創り出すことが意図された．

ポンテ・ペケーナ駅は次のようないくつかの特殊な問題を抱えていた．すなわちこの部分において400mの半径で線路がカーブを描きながら川と2本の道路を横切っていることである．プレキャストされた部材の集合で駅舎が構成されており，40mの3つのスパンが道と川をまたいでいる．

出口はプラットホームの両端にそれぞれ配置されており，川のどちらの岸にも降りられるようになっている．キャンティレバーで持ち出された階段は，視覚的に柱とうまくからみ合いながら美しい光景を創り出している．

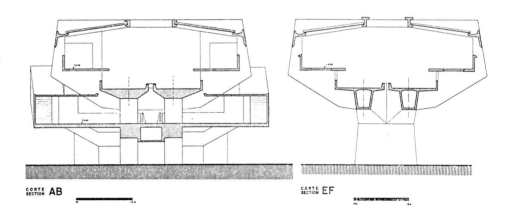

The São Paulo subway is the most important development of the last decade in the metropolis. The design intention of this project is to create an integrated structure in which the elevated section emerges from the line like an offshoot.

Ponte Pequena posed some unusual problems since that portion of the line curves at a 400m radius while transversing a river and two avenues. A set of precast elements constitute the station and three 40-meter spans bridge the roadway and the river.

Exits were placed at either end of the platform, serving both banks. The cantilevered stairways are exploited aesthetically, interacting visually with the piers.

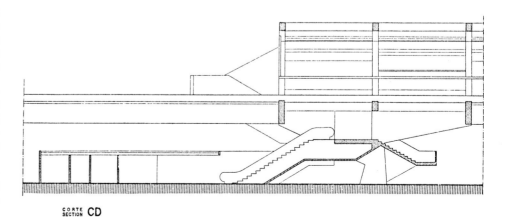

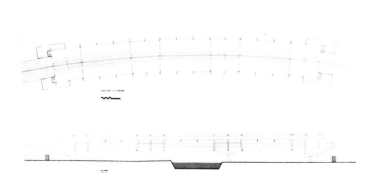

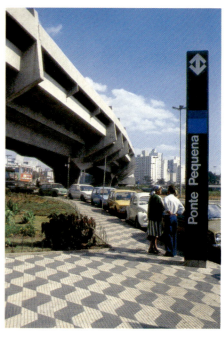

L. GUEDES RESIDENCE
São Paulo, 1971
Architect : Joaquim Guedes

L.ゲーデス邸

サンパウロ市

設計：ジョアキン・ゲーデス

この住宅の中心となる空間は，通りのレベルよりも低いところに配置されており，通りからはほとんどうかがうことができず大変控えめなものになっている．入口は通りのレベルにあり，庭は一段低いところに位置する．4本の柱に支えられたモジュールを持つプランは，長方形を基本とし一部機能的な空間によって変形されている．

構造は打放しコンクリートで，木製のサッシが使われ，また，建物のファサードはコンクリート製のひさしによって太陽光から十分に保護されている．中心の居間空間は可動のガラス戸で囲まれており，夏には大きなテラスのようにすることができる．

与えられた敷地において住み易い空間は何かという分析と，構造的な統一性を生み出すために行われた選択の結果，ここで用いられている表現手段が生み出された．

The main space of this house is located below the street level, making it almost invisible from the street and very discreet. The entrance is at street level and the garden on the lower. Supported by four columns, the modular plan is rectangular and modified by functional areas.

The structure is of exposed reinforced concrete with wooden sash. The concrete eaves adequately protect the facade from the sun. In summer the main living area, which is enclosed by moveable glass panels, is transformed into a large terrace.

The language utilized is the result of an analysis of the habitable volume on the site and a preference for constructional unity.

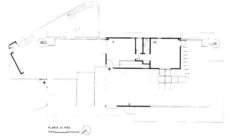
3rd floor

2nd floor

1st floor

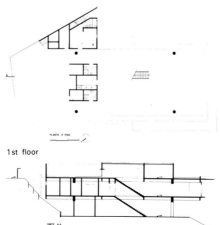
section

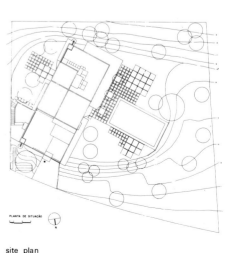
site plan

MOREAU RESIDENCE

Ibiúna, São Paulo, 1978

Architect : Joaquim Guedes

モレアウ邸

サンパウロ州イビウーナ

設計：ジョアキン・ゲーデス

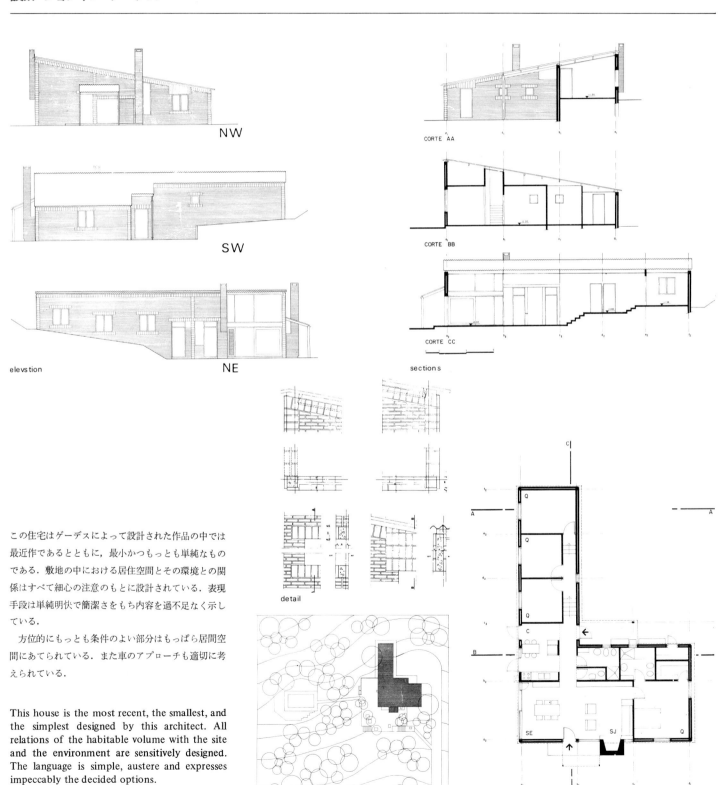

この住宅はゲーデスによって設計された作品の中では最近作であるとともに，最小かつもっとも単純なものである．敷地の中における居住空間とその環境との関係はすべて細心の注意のもとに設計されている．表現手段は単純明快で簡潔さをもち内容を過不足なく示している．

方位的にもっとも条件のよい部分はもっぱら居間空間にあてられている．また車のアプローチも適切に考えられている．

This house is the most recent, the smallest, and the simplest designed by this architect. All relations of the habitable volume with the site and the environment are sensitively designed. The language is simple, austere and expresses impeccably the decided options.

The best-oriented side is used exclusively for the living spaces; even the car access is placed in a neutral location.

BEER RESIDENCE
R. Jacupiranga, São Paulo, 1976
Architect: Joaquim Guedes

ビーエル邸

サンパウロ市ルア・ジャクピランガ

設計：ジョアキン・ゲーデス

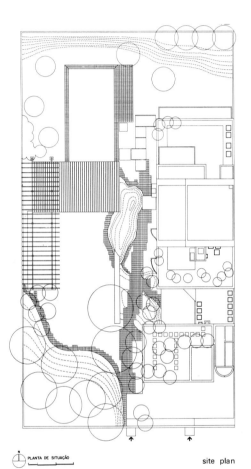
site plan

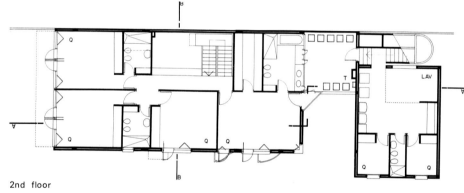
3rd floor

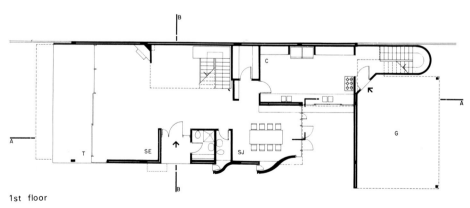
2nd floor

1st floor

敷地を含めた居住空間とそのまわりの環境そしてそれを取り巻く文化の相互関係に対する批判的な分析がこの設計の出発点であった．表現手段は厳格で欠点のないものであり，内容をよく示している．

壁は構造として扱われており，また空間の関係は十分に分析されている．コンクリートの構造体は内部にもあらわれているが，光の状態によって材料の不連続感は軽減されている．

A critical analysis of the interrelation of the inhabited volume with the site, the environment, and the culture was basic to this design. The language is severe and impeccable, expressing the decided options.

The walls are structural and the relation of volumes is carefully analysed. The concrete structure is visible on the interior where the light minimizes the material's discontinuity.

CARAIBA NEW TOWN
Caraiba, Bahia
Architect : Joaquim Guedes

カライーバ・ニュータウン
バイーア州カライーバ
設計:ジョアキン・ゲーデス

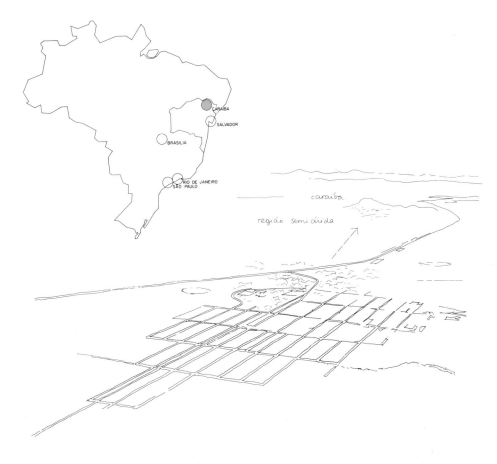

カライーバはバイーア州の降雨量の非常に少ない地域にある銅鉱山に隣接し，そこで働く技術者と労働者のために計画された人口15,000人の新都市である．計画をまとめるには，適切な概念とプログラムおよび都市構造に対する徹底的な分析が必要であった．この分析には次のような内容が含まれていた．(1)当該地域と既存市街地体系およびこの新都市のこの地域における将来の役割に対する生態地質学的システムの分析．(2)都市内の社会組織とその相互関係のシステムに対する分析，(3)環境に適した快適さを生み出すためのこの土地に特有の材料及び技術の収集．

この新都市は，隣接した地域の都市化した部分にそって拡大してゆくよう計画されている．

ここで採用されたグリッド以外の都市パターンを提案するとしたら組織構造に対する基準が不十分となったろう．それぞれの中心に一ヶ所ずつ計画された広場は，すべての都市施設の配置を構造的に組織だてている．この都市の地理上の位置によって，建築材料と空間組織および方位が決定されている．ここの土でつくられた特殊レンガが開発され，住宅の内部空間をたいへん快適にしている．

Caraiba is a new town planned for 15,000 technicians and workers attached to a copper mine in a semi-arid region of Bahia State. The project required a thorough analysis to determine an appropriate concept, program, and urban structure. This analysis included (1) the eco-geological system of the region, the existing urban hierarchy and the future regional function of the town; (2) the system of social organization within the town and its interrelationships; and (3) the enlistment of local materials and techniques for environmental comfort. The new town is expected to grow along with the urbanization of neighboring areas.

Organization criteria were not sufficient to suggest other urban patterns than the adopted grid. The plazas structurally organize the plan of all urban facilities, one plaza being at the center of each.

House construction materials, space organization and orientation are related to the location. Special bricks made of local clay were developed to maximize internal comfort within the houses.

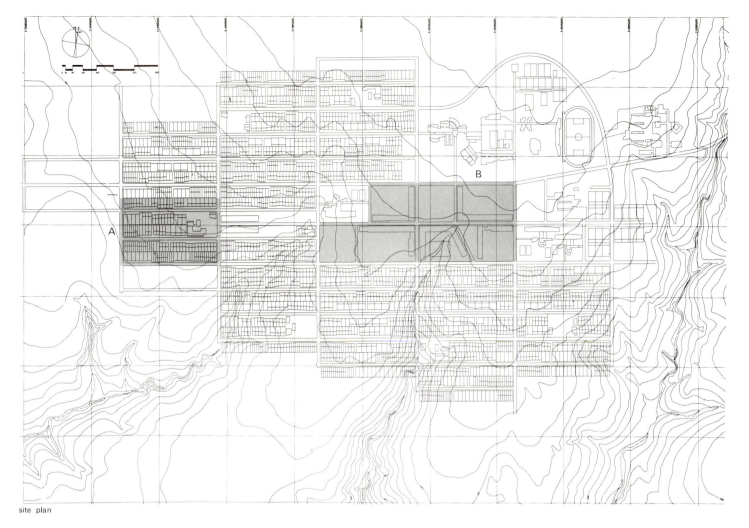
site plan

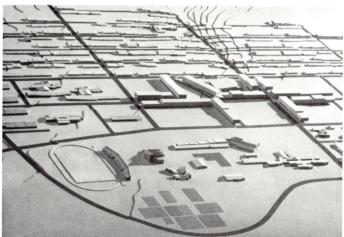

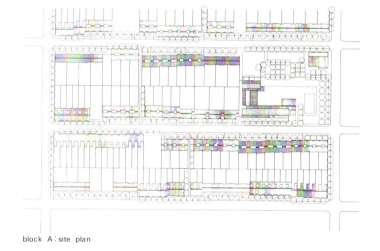
block A : site plan

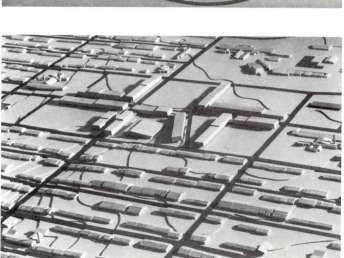

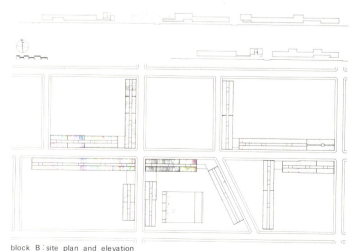
block B : site plan and elevation

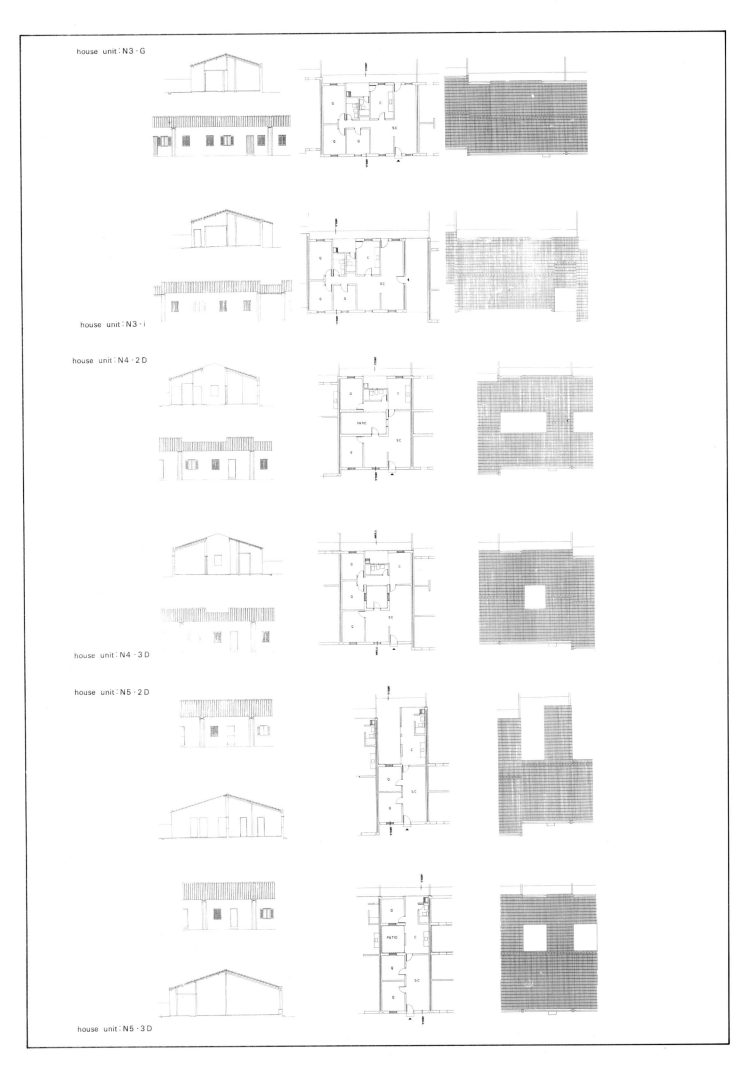

これらの写真は，ブラジル北部バイーア州の乾燥地帯の典型的な集落のパターンを示している．ポソ・デ・フォラは，カライバからおよそ30km離れた村で，そのパターンと伝統的建築は，ニュータウンの設計に対して，数多くのコンセプチュアルな要素を提供した．

These photos are from Poço-de-Fora, a typical village in the semi-arid region of Bahia State. Poço-de-Fora is located 30km away from Caraiba and its village pattern and architecture has inspired and influenced the team in elaborating the newtown's Plan.

IBM EDUCATIONAL CENTER

Gávea, Rio de Janeiro, 1973
Architect: Pontual Associados, Arquitetura e Planejamento Ltda.

IBM教育センター

リオデジャネイロ市ガヴェア

設計:ポントゥアール・アソシアドス

このIBM教育センターはガヴェアのリオ地区にあり，ここは歴史的な遺産として国の歴史美術局によって管理されている地域に含まれている．計画案は手厚く保護されてきた既存の緑を十分考慮し，建物群は自然の景観に調和するよう配置されている．

建物は福利厚生プログラムと教育プログラムのための二つのブロックで構成されている．福利厚生関係のブロックは古い農家のある場所に計画され，教育関係のブロックは湖をへだてた丘の上の平坦な場所に配置されている．そしてこの二つのブロックは設備関係の配管が組み込まれた橋で結ばれている．

5,500㎡の敷地の中には62戸のアパート，レジャーのためのエリア，ラウンジ，昼食室，管理部門，オーディトリアム，図書館，教室群が含まれている．

IBM's Educational Center is located in the Rio quarter of Gavea, designated an historical landmark by the National Historical and Artistic Monuments Agency.

The project tried to preserve the existing greenery, fitting the buildings harmoniously into the landscape. The buildings consist of two blocks, one for the social program and the other for the educational program. The social block is located on the site of an old farmhouse while the educational block is located on a flat track on a hill across a lake. A bridge links the blocks and carries the piping system.

The 5,500 square meter floor area includes 62 apartments, a leisure area and lounge, a lunch room, administration offices, an auditorium, library, and classrooms.

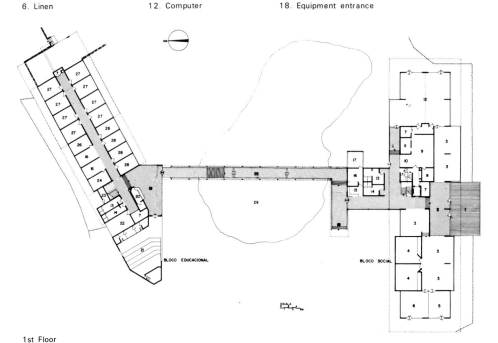

2 nd floor
1. Bedroom
2. Bathroom
3. Waiting-room
4. Medical Station
5. Nurse-room
6. Linen
7. Fan coil
8. Metallic roof
9. Terrace
10. Metallic roof
11. Computer
12. Computer
13. Toilet (man)
14. Toilet (woman)
15. Class-room (group)
16. Class-room
17. Projection-room
18. Equipment entrance

1st Floor
1. Deck
2. Lobby
3. Living room
4. TV room
5. Game room
6. Billiard room
7. Fan coil
8. Pantry
9. kitchen
10. Refrigeration room
11. Laundry
12. Restaurant
13. Toilet (man)
14. Toilet (woman)
15. Reception room
16. Secretary
17. General Manager
18. Entrance
19. Foyer
20. Bar
21. Auditorium
22. Library
23. Gas
24. Printing room
25. Bridge
26. store
27. Instructor Office
28. Manager
29. Lake

83

COSAMA RESERVOIR
Manaus, Amazonas, 1972
Architect : Severiano Mario Porto

コザーマ貯水槽

アマゾーナス州マナーウス市

設計：セベリアーノ・マリオ・ポルト

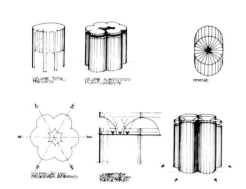

conceptual sketches

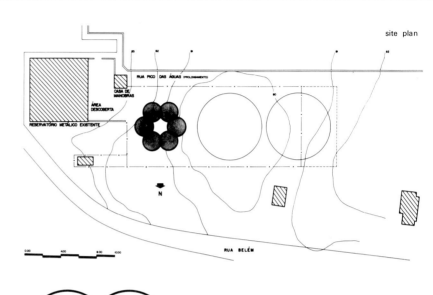

site plan

この計画はCOSAMA（マナウス公衆衛生会社）によって市街地よりはるかに高い所に建てられた六つの単位からなる貯水槽である．それゆえに街の景観に与える影響はとても大きい．

この種の設備は往々にして単一で巨大な建造物になりがちである．いくつかのシリンダーに分けるというこの考え方は，造形上の検討と同時に構造上の検討の所産である．そしてその結果スリムでエレガントな形になっている．

貯水槽は屋根の形を波状にすることですべて表面に細い溝のある打放しコンクリート造とすることができた．特殊な照明装置が光と影の織りなす効果を生み出し垂直の方向性を強調するであろう．

特別地区なのでレクリエーション施設がすぐ近くに設けられている．このプランのモチーフはこの会社のシンボルマークとして使われている．

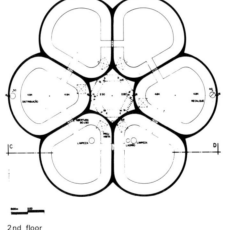

2nd floor

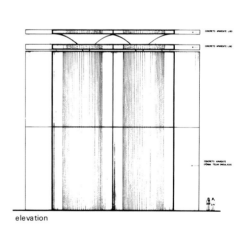

elevation

1st floor

This project is a series of five reservoirs to be constructed by COSAMA — the Sanitation Company of Manaus — on a site high above the city, and, consequently, greatly influencing the cityscape.

This type of equipment is usually constructed as a single large element. The idea of subdivision into various cylinders is the product of structural as well as plastic considerations, and results in a slim and elegant form.

The reservoir is all in exposed reinforced concrete with a striated texture obtained by using forms of corrugated plastic roofing. A special lighting system will accent the verticality by making a play of light and shadow.

Recreation areas are planned nearby because of the privileged location. The motif of the plan is used as a symbol by the company.

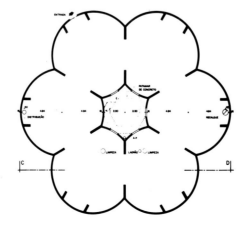

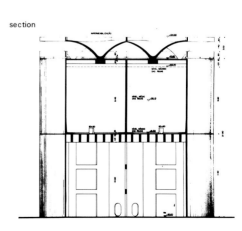

section

SHUSTER RESIDENCE
Tarumã, Amazonas
Architect: Severiano Mario Porto

シュースデル邸

アマゾーナス州タルマン

設計：セベリアーノ・マリオ・ポルト

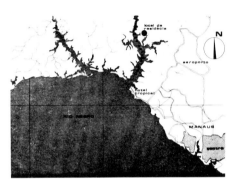
location plan

　この家は広大なアマゾン地区の細い川が流れ，密生した草木でおおわれている敷地に建っている．気候はくもりがちで地面に日光のあたることはない．日中の気温と湿度は高いが夜間になると寒いほどである．敷地には無数の木が生えておりそのため木の葉が厚くカーペットのように地表をおおい，それが堆肥となる．この家の持主は，地誌学者夫妻であるが，できるだけこの土地に手をいれないことを望んでいた．彼らの生活様式は単純なものだったので空間的にも材料の点でも一般に考えられるよりもずっと自由な構成をとることができた．

　床と壁をはじめとする構造材にはすべて地方的な道具と技術による木組が用いられた．土地の特性を生かして土壌のつりあいを保つようにできるだけ建坪を減らした．生活の領域が中央部の空間をとりかこみ，またそれらは自然の通風が可能なように配慮されている．

This house is located on a large rural lot in the Amazon region, on a bank of a narrow river covered with dense vegetation. The weather is cloudy and the sun does not reach the soil. The temperature and humidity are high during the day but it is cold at night. There are a large number of trees on the site which are responsible for a thick carpet of leaves and compost on the ground. The owners of the house, a topographer and his wife, preferred to leave as much of the site undisturbed as possible. Their simple lifestyle permitted spaces and materials to be organized freely rather than in a traditional order.

All structure, floors and walls are made of lumber worked with local tools and techniques. Utilizing the site's peculiarities, a minimum area of the soil is covered in order to maintain soil equilibrium.

The living areas surround a central space and are open to natural ventilation.

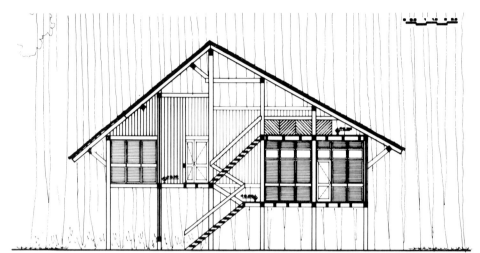
section 1-1

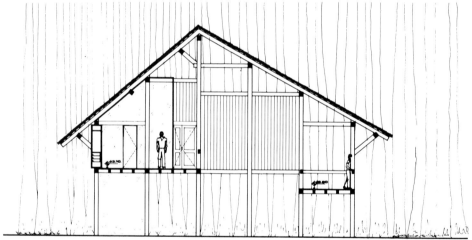
section 2-2

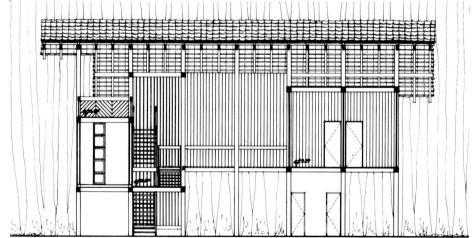
section 3-3

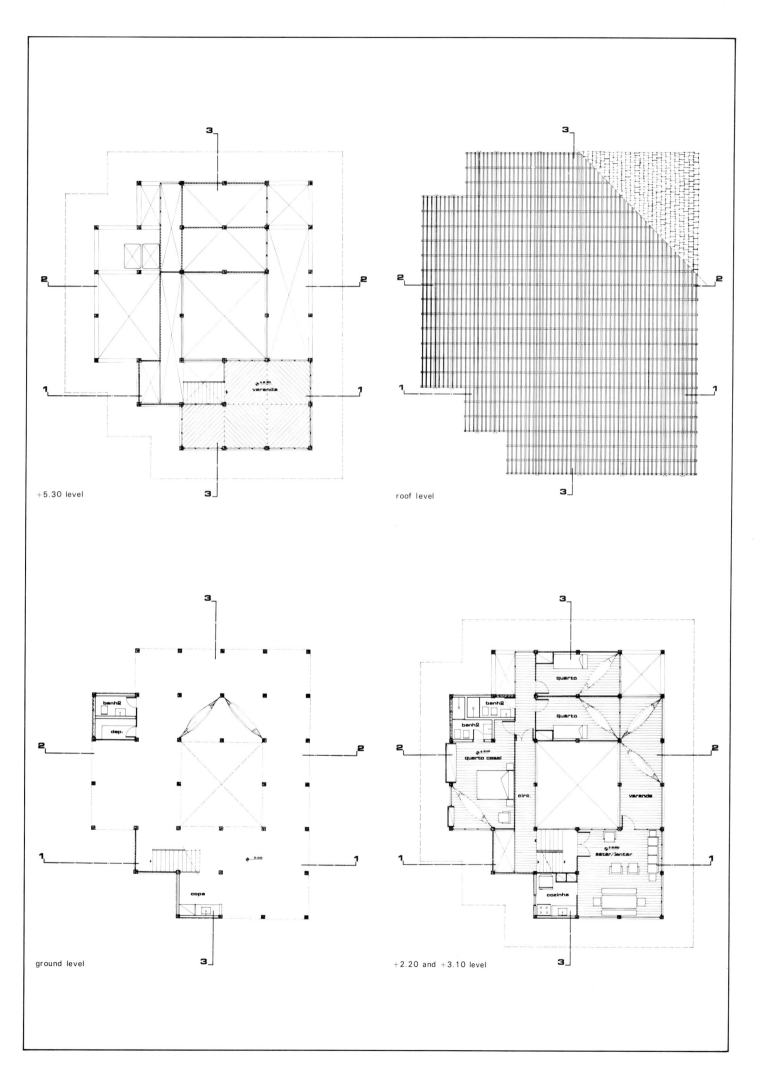

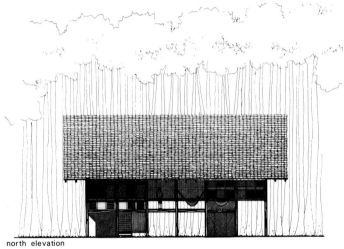
north elevation

east elevation

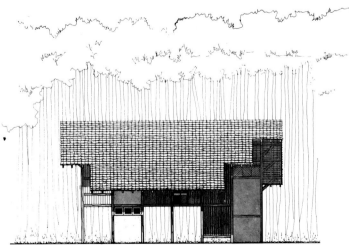
south elevation

PORTO RESIDENCE
Manaus, Amazonas, 1971
Architect: Severiano Mario Porto

ポルト邸
アマゾーナス州マナウス市
設計：セベリアーノ・マリオ・ポルト

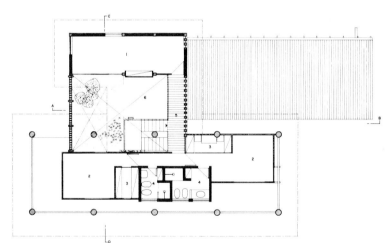

1 private living
2 bedrooms
3 closet
4 bathroom
5 corridor
6 void of the living

1 hall
2 living
3 cafeteria. TV set
4 dining room
5 Private verandah
6 internal path
7 toilet
8 kitchen
9 facilities
10 storage
11 maid's room
12 bathroom
13 car parking

elevations

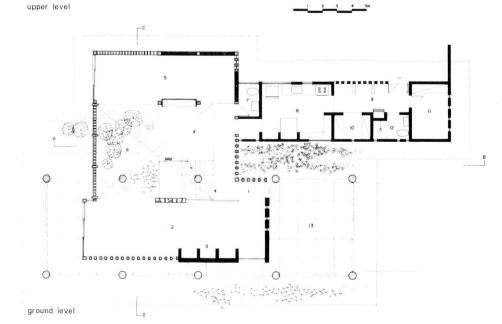

upper level

ground level

自分自身の家を設計し建設するにあたり，この建築家は単に生態学的な配慮だけではなく敷地と建物を一体化するような解決法を生み出そうと試みた．

彼はこの地方で長い経験をつみそして地域特性をよく理解しているので，原住民たちが伝統的な道具を使ってつくるこの地方特有の木組を用いて家をつくった．使用された木は，イタウバ，マカランドゥバ，スクピラ，セドロ，アグアノ，ロウロ，アリトゥ，マカカウバなどである．

プランは中央の庭を囲むように延びている．二重の天井と通風のための細長いすき間はこの地方の気候のもとでは必要なものであるが，同時に目を楽しませる要素ともなっている．

この地方特産の材料と環境条件を尊重すること，そして現代の技術は用いていないということがこの計画を確かなものにしている．

In designing and constructing his own house, the architect tried to achieve a solution that goes beyond ecological considerations and integrates the building with the site.

Taking advantage of his long experience in the region and his understanding of local peculiarities, local lumber worked by natives with traditional tools was used for the construction. The woods used include Itauba, Macaranduba, Sucupira, Cedro, Aguano, Louro Aritu, and Macacauba.

The plan develops around a central garden. The double ceiling and ventilation slits required by the climate become a pleasing visual element.

The native materials, the respect for the environment, and she absence of contemporary techniques are the hallmarks of this project.

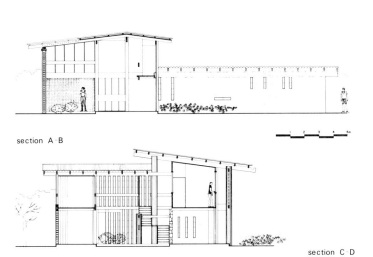

section A-B

section C-D

ZANETTINI RESIDENCE

Pereiras, Atibaia, São Paulo, 1975
Architect: Siegbert Zanettini

ザネチーニ邸

サンパウロ州アチバイア市ペレイラス

設計：シーギベルチ・ザネチーニ

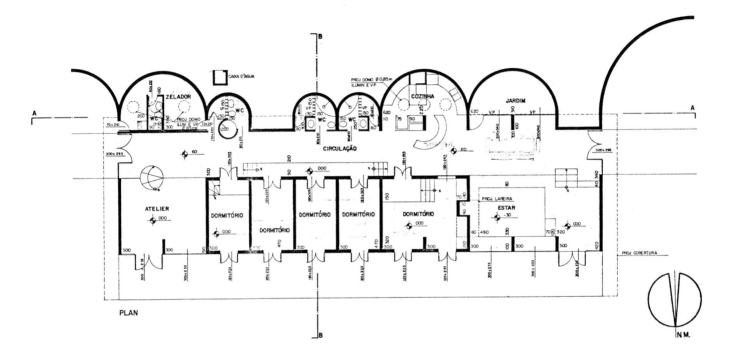

PLAN

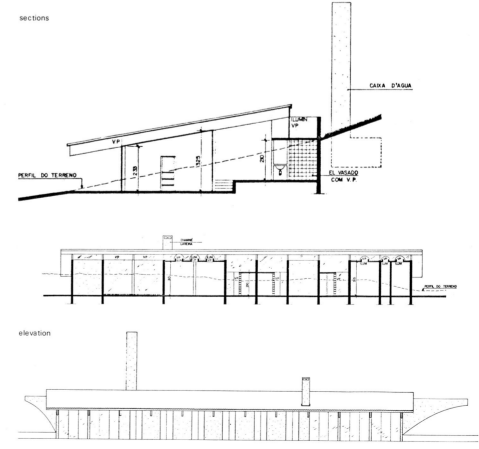

sections

elevation

この計画では建築家は，環境及び建物と周囲の景観とのつり合いを重んじて景観そのものを造形している．どの空間においても緑樹が常に主要な要素であり，この家に視覚的な一貫性を与えている．この家はまた，両側にある広場に向かう中心軸にそって構成されている．

この家の構造を支えるために丘の斜面が切りとられた．土地固有の植物は土地の雰囲気を醸し出すために使われている．主構造はこの地方の粘土でつくられた素朴なレンガと木材である．適切な採光と通風を得るために木製の格子戸が用いられ，正面にはゆったりとしたベランダが設けられている．

The architect models the landscape in this project, respecting the environment and the equilibrium between the building and the surrounding landscape. Greenery is a constant element in all spaces and visually completes the house, which is organized along a central axis that flows into two lateral plazas. The sloped hillside was cut to support the structure of the house.

Indigenous plantings are used for a local feel. The major construction materials are simple brick, fabricated from the local clay, and wood. Wooden latticed doors are provided for adequate light and ventilation. The front facade has a generous veranda.

BANESPA TUTOIA BANK

Paraizo, São Paulo, 1978
Architect: Siegbert Zanettini

バネスパ・ツトイア銀行

サンパウロ市パライーゾ

設計：シーギベルチ・ザネチーニ

site plan

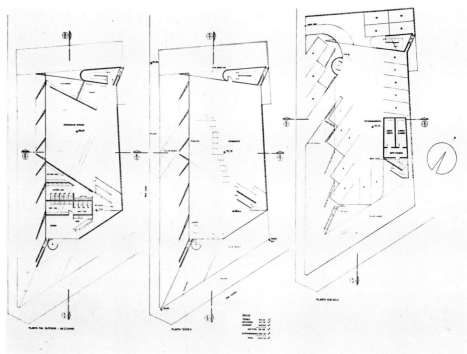

floor plans

都心部に位置するため，この銀行のデザインにはブラジルの現代建築と歴史的なつながりを与えられている．構造そのものは内容空間を規定しているが，柱はブリーズ・ソレイユの形に変えられ，同時に軸的方向性を建物に与えている．

銀行内部での活動が多岐にわたるため，固定的な空間の分割は行われていない．この結果生じた流動性によって，将来の増築に対する適応性を備えた空間が生まれた．

地上階がパブリックな活動のために使われている一方，上階は管理部門のために使われている．16台分の駐車場が地下につくられている．

Located on an urban site, this bank's design is related historically to modern Brazilian architecture. The structure proper defines the enclosed space; columns are transformed to brise-soleils and give the building an axial orientation at the same time.

Diversification of activities within the bank eliminates rigid division of spaces. The resulting fluidity allows the necessary space flexibility for future adaptations.

The ground level is for public activities while the upper is for administration. Parking for 16 cars is provided below ground.

HOSPITAL FOR THE HANDICAPPED

Brasília, 1976
Architect: João Filgueiras Lima

身体障害者のための病院

ブラジリア

設計:ジョアオ・フィウゲイラス・リーマ

身体障害者のためのこの病院はブラジルの社会経済的な状況に適した医療サービスを行う技術者を訓練する目的で創設された.より低いコストとよりよいサービスを達成する最新の技術をひろめていくためには,今までブラジルで作られたことのない装置類を導入することが必要である.それゆえこの病院の研究所は,このような装置を開発するという重要な役割を担っている.それには,技術的なノウハウが要求されると同時に,いろいろな問題の革新的な解決策を見つけるためのブラジル的な条件を理解する必要があるだろう.

建築的な概念を導く全体の方針は次のようなものである.

(1) 予想される絶え間ない大量の交通を処理する統一的な構造を生み出すための既存建物との相互連絡の方法.
(2) 固定した設備と技術に基づいたプログラムは当然変更の可能性があり,それによって必要とされる建設方法の柔軟性と発展性.
(3) 屋外訓練をするために必要な治療上の雰囲気をつくり出す景観的配慮のほどこされたオープンスペースの創出.
(4) 自然光と快適な温度.

内部のサーキュレーションの問題を解決するため,6mに及ぶ敷地の高低差を利用して3層の建物がつくられた.各階は部分的にしか重なっていないので,ある場所には庭園化したテラスを創る必要があった.

建設費の低減と施工に要する日数を減らし,かつ仕上の質を保つために,プレファブ工法が提案された.これらの要素はテラス,設備用配管,照明や換気のために,交換できるような形で使用されている.

次にあげる都市的な処理が行われている.(1)都市道路網に対し2本のアクセス路を創り出したこと,(2)計画的な交通システムと内部のゾーニング.(3)自動車交通の影響をやわらげるための密度の高い緑地帯の創出.

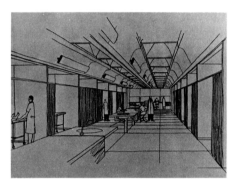

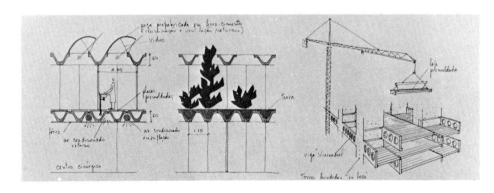

This hospital for the handicapped was created to train technicians for medical service adapted to the socio-economic conditions of Brazil. The introduction of modern techniques to achieve lower cost and better service depends on equipment not yet made in Brazil. The hospital's workshop, then, assumes a significant role in producing such equipment; it will require both mechanical know-how and an understanding of Brazilian conditions to find innovative solutions to their problems.

The general principals defining the architectural concept are as follows.
– Interconnection with the existing building to create a unified structure for the constant and heavy traffic anticipated.
– Flexibility and expandability of the construction necessitated by the natural fragility of programs based on fixed equipment and technology.
– Creation of landscaped open space to provide a therapeutic atmosphere for open-air exercise. Natural lighting and thermal comfort.

Three stories were created to solve the problems of internal circulation by taking advantage of the six meter variation of contour on the site. The partial superposition of these floors made necessary the creation of artificially gardened terraces.

Prefabricated construction was proposed to reduce the cost and time of construction and to assure the quality of finish. These elements are used interchangeably to create terraces, to house equipment tubes, or for lighting and ventilation.

Urban treatment consisted of (1) establishing two means of access to the urban road system; (2) a programmed traffic system and internal zoning; and (3) creation of a zone of dense greenery to buffer the effects of vehicular traffic.

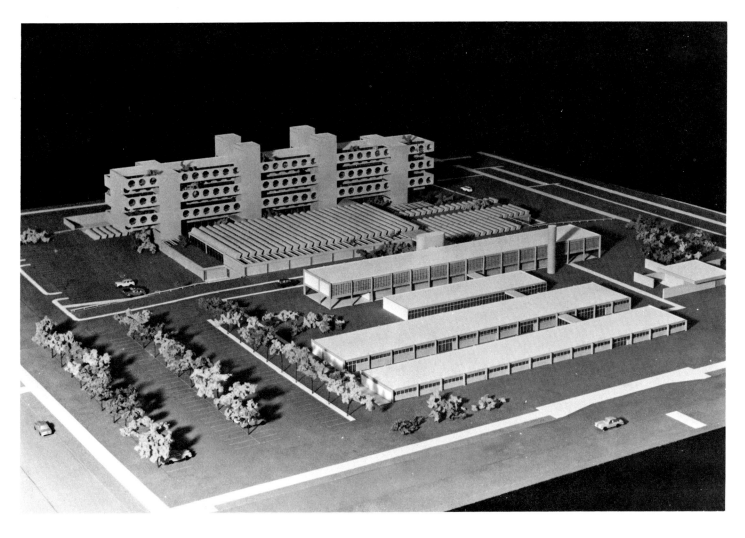

section

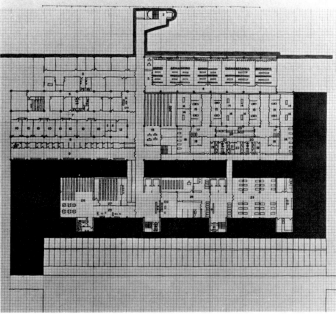
−3.50 level

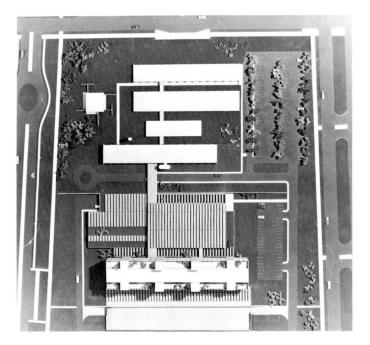

99

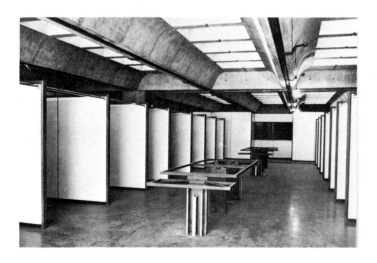

ADMINISTRATIVE CENTER OF BAHIA

Salvador, Bahia
Architect : João Filgueiras Lima

バイーア州行政センター

バイーア州サルバドール市

設計：ジョアオ・フィウゲイラス・リーマ

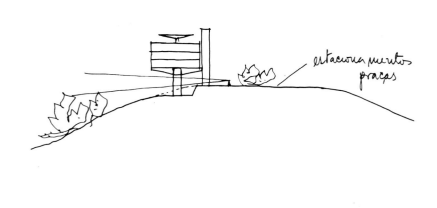

飛行場に近接しているという条件によってこの州の行政センターは長く低いデザインになった．最終案はまわりの景観に合わせて地上から浮き上がった構造を持つ．

　将来における建物の拡張を可能にし，短期的観点からは体系的できちっとした解決を引き出すために，明解な構造システムが創り出された．地形のカーブに沿って曲っているコンクリート製のプラットホームが，拡張可能で柔軟性に富んだオフィス階を形成するプレファブ化された部材のシステムを支えている．維持管理用のダクトシステムは，通信システムの進歩や他の作業の自動化に必要な量を予想してつくられている．

　ファサードの方向が様々なのは元の地形を尊重したからである．適切な自然換気と，日照調節の工夫によって空調システムをはぶくことが可能である．中央部に設けられた中空の部分が煙突効果を発揮して全体の換気を行っている．開口部は横引きの強化ガラスとグラスファイバー製の可動ブリーズ・ソレイユから成る．

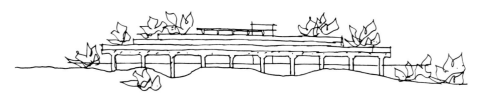

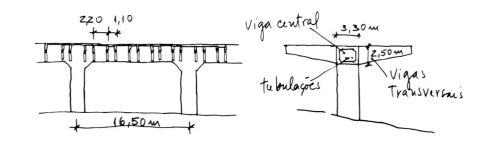

The proximity of an airport led to a long, low design for this state administrative center. The result is an elevated structure which conforms to the landscape.

　A distinct structural system was created to enable lengthening of the building in the future and also to induce a systematic and disciplined solution in the short run. A concrete platform, following the curves of the topography, supports a system of prefabricated elements creating extendable and flexible office floors. A maintainance duct system is provided in anticipation of the necessity to modernize the communications system and automatization of other processes.

　The orientation of the facade in various directions is a concession to the original landscape. The elimination of an air conditioning system is possible because of adequate natural ventilation and sun/shade design. Cross ventilation is obtained by utilizing chimney action in the central open well. Sash consists of sliding tempered glass and movable fiberglass brise-soleil.

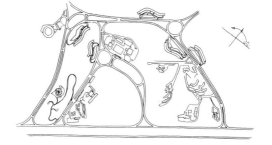

102

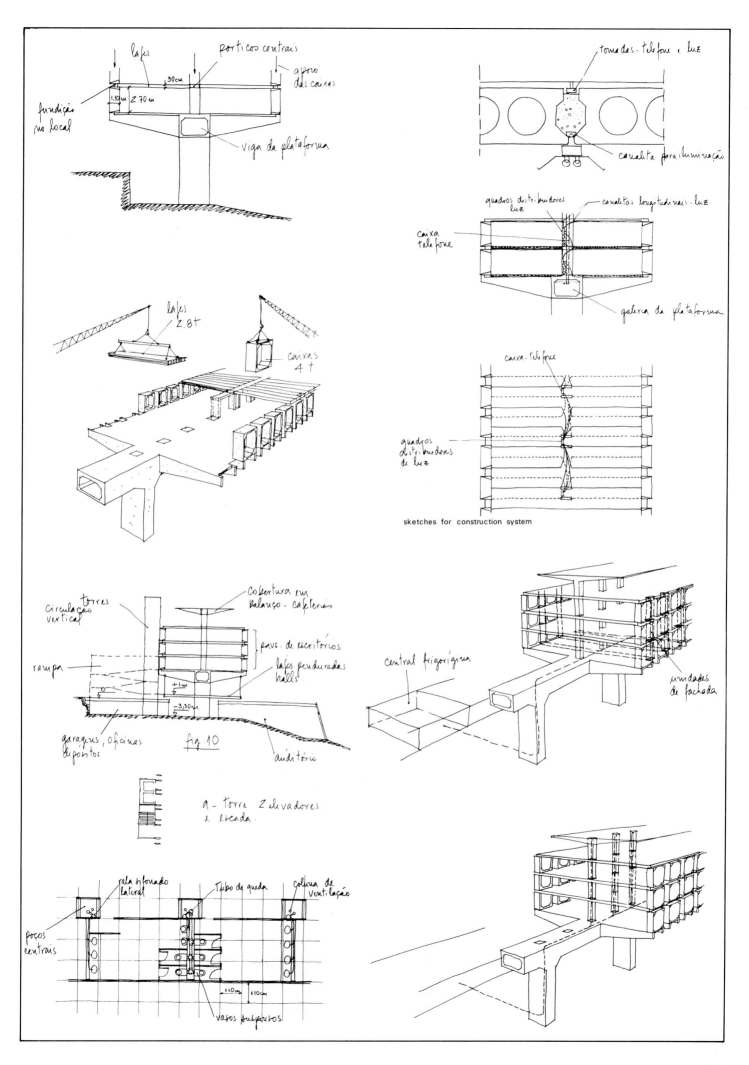

sketches for construction system

CAB CHAPEL
Salvador, Bahia, 1974
Architect : João Filgueiras Lima

CABチャペル

バイーア州サルバドール市

設計：ジョアオ・フィウゲイラス・リーマ

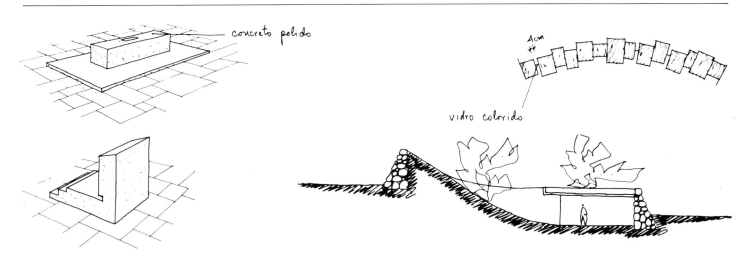

自然景観の美しさをそのまま残そうという願望がこの設計の基本的な部分として役立っている。サルバドール市はいろいろなデザイナーたちを啓発してきた文化的・宗教的な伝統を持つ歴史的な都市である。

洗礼場とチャペルは，敷地の中にひかえめな軟らかい外形を描きながら建っている。花弁状のコンクリートの構造体がらせん形に上昇し，主身廊では主要な視覚的要素を形成している。そして自然光を採り入れるための隙間が花弁の間にある屋根の線にまで延びている。

内部は打放しコンクリートと木で構成され，簡素な雰囲気がただよっており，単純ではあるが，カソリックのチャペルにふさわしい壮重さを備えている。床はごく自然に取り扱われ，コロニアル様式の教会に似た石の壁は，さまざまな材料の可能性を試みている空間にまとまりを与えている。

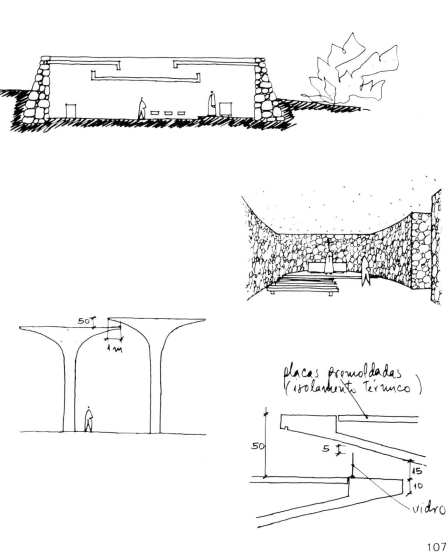

A desire to preserve the natural beauty of the landscape served as the basis for this design. Salvador is an historical city with a cultural and religious tradition that has inspired various designers.

The baptistery and chapel lie discreetly and softly outlined in the site. An ascendental helicoid of structural concrete petals constitutes the single visual element in the main nave; slits for natural lighting penetrate the roofline between the petals.

The interior is austere, consisting of exposed concrete and wood. Although simple, it provides a dignity appropriate to a Catholic chapel. The ground is treated naturally and the stone walls in the manner of colonial churches, organizing a space which explores all possibilities of the construction materials.

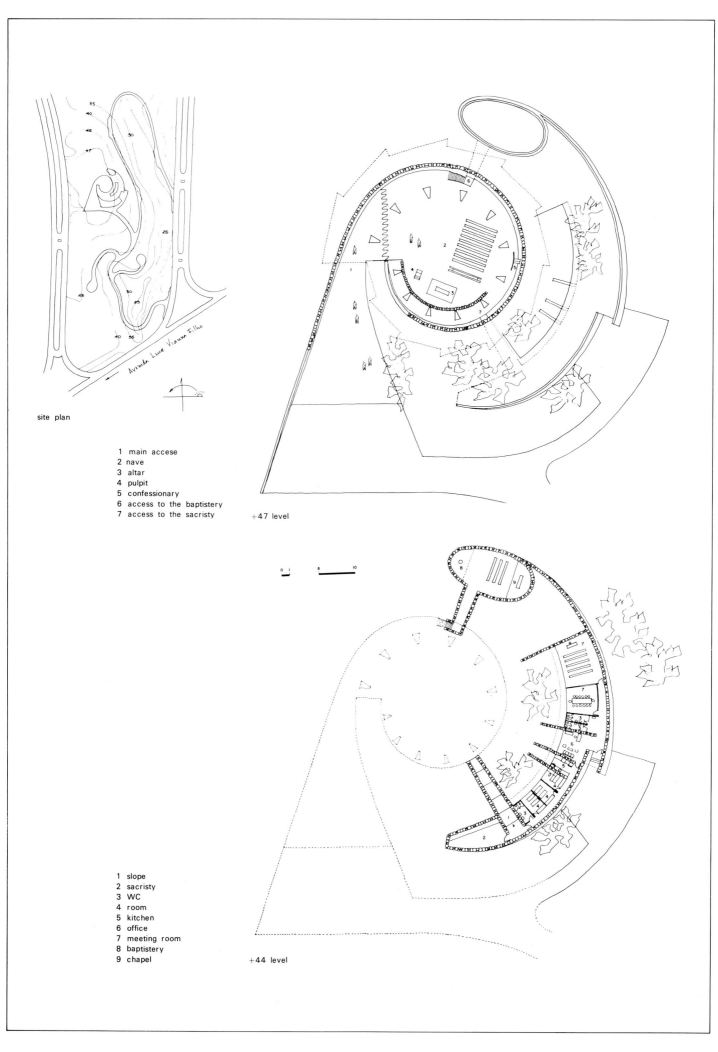

site plan

1 main accese
2 nave
3 altar
4 pulpit
5 confessionary
6 access to the baptistery
7 access to the sacristy

+47 level

1 slope
2 sacristy
3 WC
4 room
5 kitchen
6 office
7 meeting room
8 baptistery
9 chapel

+44 level

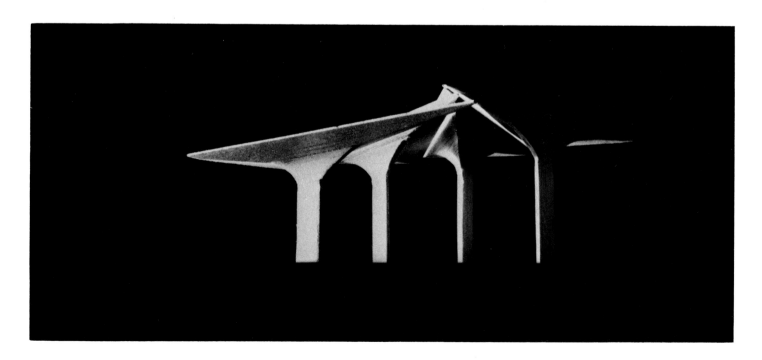

MIGUEL DE CERVANTES HIGH SCHOOL

Morumbi, São Paulo, 1978
Architect : Rino Levi

ミゲウ・デ・セルバンテス校

サンパウロ市 モルンビー

設計：リーノ・レーヴィ

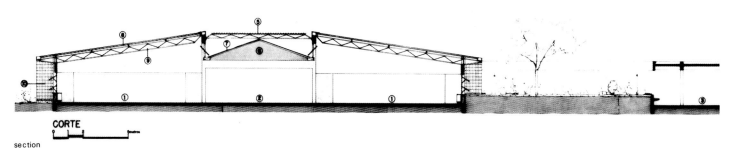

section

1 classroom
2 teaching materials
6 covered playground
4 distribution
5 shading perforated roofing tile
6 wired glass
7 transparent glass
8 plastified roofing
9 steel structure
10 red brick
11 perforated roofing tile
12 "pistofibra": a treated glass wool
13 glass wool
14 asphalted cardboard

detail

この学校は敷地面積56,850㎡，延床面積17,000㎡の規模を持ち，スペイン人社会の主唱によって建設された．ここではオープン・プランの建築に，実験的な試みと新制度を組み合せて質の高い教育を行うことが意図された．

不整方形敷地に，屋根付きの通路で連絡された4つの主要なブロックが有機的に連続しながら配置されている．教室棟は中央にバルコニーのある十字形のプランで構成されており，研究所，スポーツ・センター，そしてその他の必要施設が他のブロックを形成している．このプランは多目的空間に自然光と十分な通風を保証している．屋根と天井の構造は単なるおおいとしてではなく吸音および断熱層として働くよう特にデザインされている．

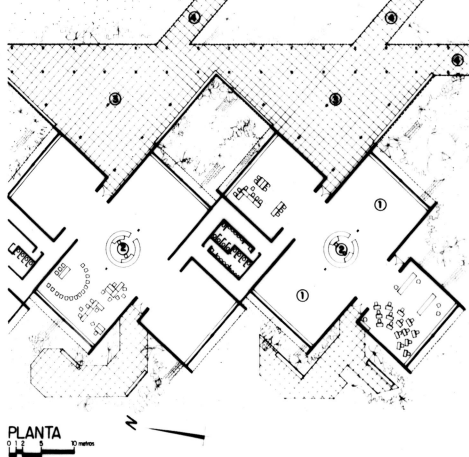

This school, with a total floor area of 17,000 square meters on a site of 56,850 square meters was built on the initiative of the Spanish community. It is intended to offer a high level of education supported by open-plan architecture, combining experimentation and innovation.

The irregular site is occupied by a continuous organic form of four main blocks linked by covered walks. The classroom block is organized in a cross pattern with a balcony in the center. A laboratory, sports center, and supporting facilities occupy the remaining blocks.

The plan provides efficient ventilation and natural lighting in the multipurpose spaces. The roof and ceiling construction was especially designed to serve as an accoustic and thermal isolator as well as schelter.

CAETANO DE CAMPOS TRAINING SCHOOL

Aclimacão, São Paulo, 1976
Architect: Croce, Aflalo & Gasperini

カエターノ・デ・カンポス校

サンパウロ市アクリマソン

設計：クロッチェ，アフラーロ＆ガスペリーニ

カエターノ・デ・カンポス州立大学は以前はサンパウロの中心街にあった伝統ある公立学校である．サンパウロ州の学校建設組合（CONESP）主催で基本構想を求めるコンペが行われ，この計画が入選した．

この学校の生徒数は2,200人にのぼり，そのプログラムは幅広く，教員養成のための施設や幼稚園および若い学生のための施設を備えている．この学校は4種の基本的な部分の複合として機能し，各部分はすべて屋根つき廊下でつながれている．

その一つは幼稚園で，独立した平屋建てとして建てられている．それは円形をしていて構内への出入口に近く位置し，主要な建物とはガラスで被われた廊下でつながっている．

第2番目の部分は学校の中心部で，教室，研究室，管理部分，図書室，教育学センター，美術室，身障者のための特別室，屋根のないプレイグラウンドと屋根付きのもの，学生食堂，管理人の寮から成る．3階の建物はランプと階段でつながれ，中心にあるサーキュレーションのための空間は巨大なドーム形の構造でおおわれている．

第3番目の部分は550人を収容できる設備のととのった劇場である．

第4番目の部分は敷地の一番低い所に位置し，体育館，着替え室，協同組合を含んでいる．

Caetano de Campos State College is a traditional public school formerly located in downtown São Paulo. The company for School Buildings of the State of São Paulo – CONESP – sponsored a competition for the preliminary

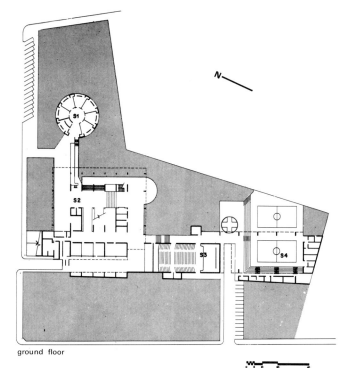

ground floor

four basic sections, all linked by covered walks.
Section 1 is the kindergarten, built as a separate, single-story building. Circular in shape, it is located near street access and is linked through a glass-covered walk to the main building.
Section 2 houses the central body of the school: classrooms, laboratories, administration concept design and this project was the winner.

The program for this school of 2,200 students is comprehensive, including facilities for children and young people as well as for teacher-training. It functions as a complex of areas, library, pedagogical center, museum, special rooms for handicapped students, open and sheltered playgrounds, a canteen and the caretaker's apartment. The three stories are linked by ramps and staircases, and the central circulation space is sheltered by a huge dome-shaped structure.
Section 3 houses a fully-equipped 550-seat auditorium.
Section 4, located at the site's lowest point, holds a covered sports gymnasium, dressing rooms, and fraternity facilities.

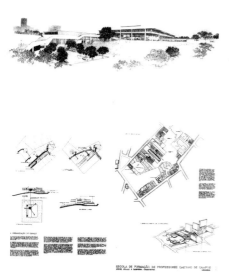

CEESP TIRADENTES BANK

Av. Tiradentes, São Paulo, 1977
Architect: Croce, Aflalo & Gasperini

セエスピ・チラデンテス銀行

サンパウロ市

設計：クロッチェ，アフラーロ＆ガスペリーニ

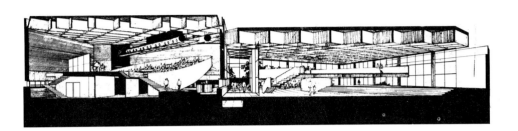

この銀行は，地下鉄南北線が走っていて市の中でも重要な道路であるチラデンテス通りに面している．面積7,500㎡におよぶ敷地は，下町にほど近い都市再開発地区の一部であり，いくつかの公共の文化施設がこの囲りに建ち並んでいる．

この場所には1851年以来の歴史を持つ刑務所が建っていた．そして通りをへだてたところには，古い僧院を利用したアルテ・サークラ博物館があり，ほんの少し離れたところはルス駅に面した由緒ある広大なルス公園がひろがっている．

建坪は5,400㎡で，その中には銀行およびその関連施設，駐車場と400席の劇場がある．動線システムは，中心の広場から放射状に拡がり施設を結びつけている小路であり，これはまた隣接する広場の自然なつながりとして，新しい建物を風景の中にとけこませるのに役立っている．

取り壊された刑務所の記念として，古い入口の門と壁の一部がランドマークとして保存された．

また，この敷地の中にはチラデンテス地下鉄駅の出口がある．

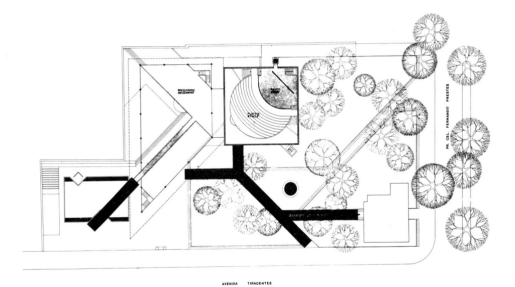

mezzanine

This bank is located on Tiradentes Avenue, an important approach corridor of the city under which runs the north-south Metro line. The 7,500 m² site is part of an urban renewal area near downtown, and is surrounded by several of the city's cultural facilities.

The site was formerly occupied by a penitentiary dating from 1851. Across the street is the Arte Sacra Museum, housed in an old monastery, and a few meters away is Luz Park, a huge old park that faces the Luz railway station.

The built area is 5,400 m², including the bank, its facilities, parking and a 400-seat theater. The circulation system is a network of internal paths, radiating from a central square, inserting the new building in the scenery as a natural extension of the neighboring square.

As a reference to the demolished penitentiary building, the old entrance gate and part of the wall were preserved as a landmark.

The site also contains the Tiradentes subway station exit.

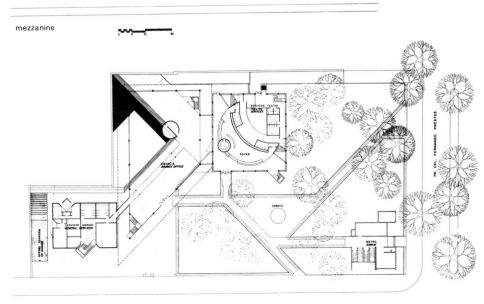

ground floor

IGUATMI BUILDING
Av. Faria Lima, São Paulo, 1973
Architect: Croce, Aflalo & Gasperini

イグアテミー・ビルディング

サンパウロ市

設計: クロッチェ, アフラーロ & ガスペリーニ

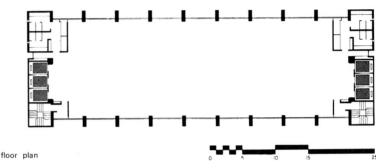

typical floor plan

この20階建ての建物は，市の南西部にあって商業地域としてにぎわっているファリア・リーマ通りに建っている．

　市条例の制約と地盤の状態により，すそひろがりの基部を持つ一風変わった形が生まれた．巨大な岩盤が地盤面よりほんの数メートル下に発見され，そのために地下にガレージを設けることが不可能になった．

　建物を逆Y字形にすることにより，2層のショッピング・スペースと2基の車輛用エレベータ付きの駐車場4層を設けることが可能となった．駐車場の上には14層の事務所とさらに一部中2階のある2層ふきぬけのペントハウスがのっている．

　基準階は面積780㎡の短形のプランで，建物の両端にはエレベータ，便所，階段等のサービス関係のエリアを含むコンクリートの箱状コアが配置されている．

This 20-floor building is located at Faria Lima Avenue, a busy commercial corridor in the southwest of the city.

The peculiar form, a tower with an enlarged base, results from municipal code restraints and subsoil conditions at the site. An enormous rock was found a few meters below ground level, making it impossible to construct basement garages.

The Y-shape provides space to house two floors of shopping and four of parking reached by two car elevators. The garage levels are topped by 14 office floors and a penthouse with a two-story open space and partial mezzanine.

The typical floor has a rectangular 780 m² plan, with a structural concrete box enveloping the service area, including elevators, toilets and staircases, in both extremities.

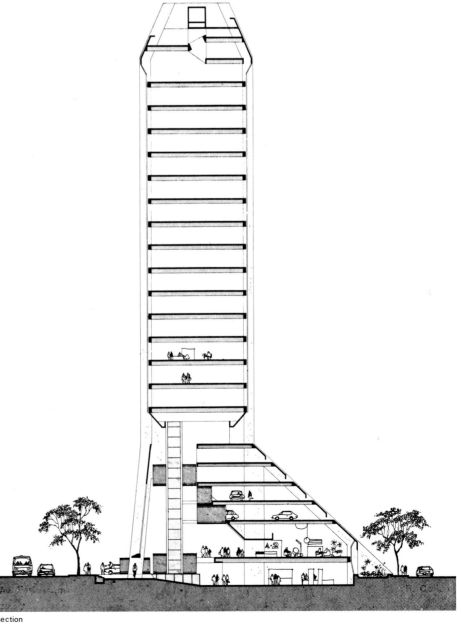

section

123

CAMPOS DO JORDÃO HALL
Campos do Jordão, São Paulo, 1978
Architect: Croce, Aflalo & Gasperini

カンポス・ド・ジョルドン・ホール

サンパウロ州カンポス・ド・ジョルドン

設計：クロッチェ，アフラーロ＆ガスペリーニ

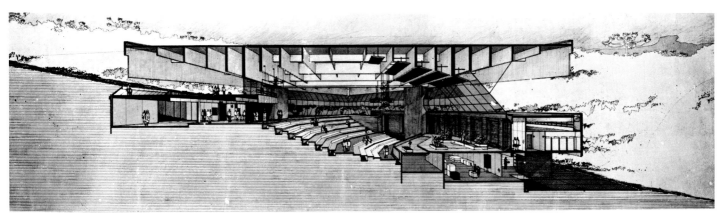
section

このホールはカンポス・ド・ジョルドンで毎年行われるウィンター・ミュージック・フェスティヴァルのために建設された．計画では，ホールの内部空間からその周囲の外部空間への変化に主要な関心がはらわれた．もとの地形はできるだけ残し，不必要な土工事は最少限におさえるという方針を建築家は採用している．

建物は周囲の景色を眺めることのできる透明なガラスの壁面を持ち，4本の柱で支持された大きな方形の板として計画された．ホワイエは屋根のある遊歩道ともいうべきものになっており，また外部にも人を受け入れる空間が意識的に配置されている．

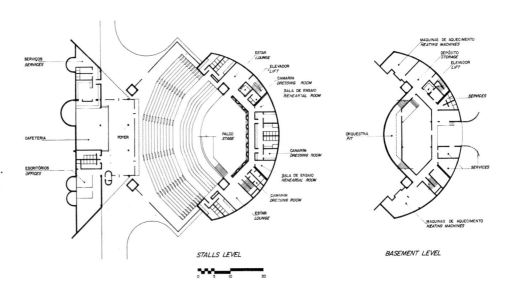

This hall was constructed for a Winter Music Festival which takes place annually at Campos do Jordão. The initial concern of the project was the transition from the sheltered space of the hall to the open space of its environment. The architects chose to preserve the original landscape and avoid unnecessary earthworks as much as possible.

The building was conceived as a large square slab supported by four columns with a transparent glass wall offering a view of the surrounding area. The foyer forms an esplanade under the roof slab; external reception areas are strategically placed on the site.

SIGRIST RESIDENCE
Morumbi, São Paulo, 1976
Architect: Eduardo de Almeida

シーグリスチ邸

サンパウロ州モルンビー

設計：エドゥアルド・デ・アウメイダ

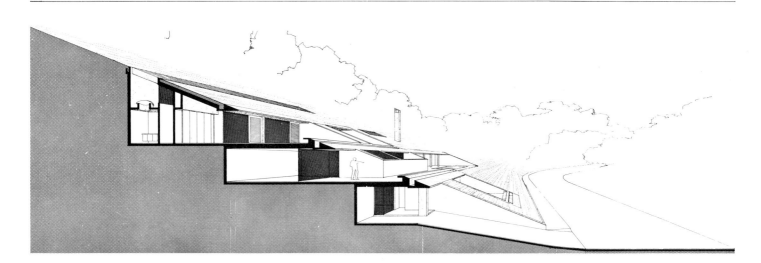

3人の息子を持つ夫婦および彼らの来客のために設計されたこの家の全体的な概念は，急勾配の敷地条件から生み出された．その基本となる考え方は丘の外観をそのままにしておき視覚的に障害となるものは作らないという方針であった．

この住宅は敷地の勾配に沿って，植栽のほどこされたスラブを，階段状に配置した3層のレベルで構成されている．植栽のほどこされた屋根はそれぞれの階にあるテラスによってとぎれており，そこから自然光を採り入れることができ，また屋外生活の場ともなり，まわりの景色を楽しむことができる．

玄関とサービス関係の施設が1階におかれ，2階には居間空間と厨房，そして3階には寝室関係の諸室が配置されている．

壁で囲まれた空間で光を必要とするところにはトップライトが設けられている．

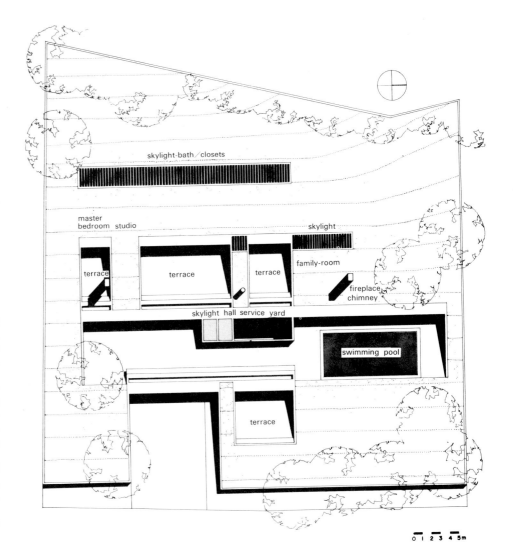

The steep sloping site suggested the general concept of this house, designed for a couple, three boys, and their guests. The basic idea was to keep the profile of the hill intact and avoid any visual obstruction.

The dwelling consists of three levels arranged as a sloping series of gardened slabs fitted to the site. The gardened roof is interupted on each floor by terraces which provide natural lighting, outdoor living space, and a view of the surrounding scenery.

On the first floor are located the general access and service areas; on the second floor, living space and kitchen; on the third floor, sleeping areas.

Space enclosed by retaining walls are skylit wherever necessary.

ALMEIDA RESIDENCE

São Paulo, 1977
Architect : Eduardo de Almeida

アウメイダ邸

サンパウロ

設計：エドゥアルド・デ・アウメイダ

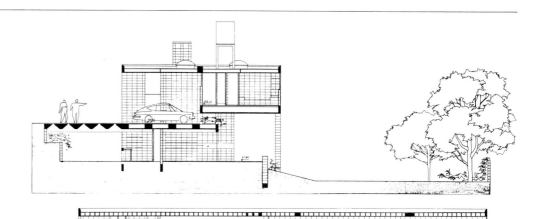

この家は5人の子供（女2人男3人）を持つ夫婦と彼らの祖母のために設計された．

　道路からのプライバシーを守ると同時に屋外での生活空間を最大限に生かすため，傾斜のある敷地が積極的に活用された．道路側の立面は閉じた壁として扱われており，人も車も橋を通って道路に出るようになっている．

　斜路と階段によって結びつけられた層状をなす空間構成は，敷地の形状と機能的な要求から導き出された．最上階には寝室関係の諸室とスタジオがおかれ，道路のレベルにはカーポートがあり，そして道路と庭の中間階には居間と洗濯室が配置され，庭と接する階には食堂，厨房およびレクリエーションのための部屋が設けられている．

　居間空間と屋外のレジャー空間は上の階が張り出しているので裏側の立面には余分な日ざしがあたらないようになっている．

This house was designed for a couple with five children — two girls and three boys — and their grandmother.

The sloping site was to be used to provide maximum outdoor living areas as well as necessary privacy from the street. The street facade has been treated as a closed wall, linked to the street by a bridge for both cars and pedestrians.

Site shape and functional requirements led to a spatial organization in levels, connected by ramps and stairs. On the upper level are sleeping areas and a studio; at street level, a carport; living room and laundry on an intermediate level; and dining, kitchen and recreation on the garden level.

Living space and outdoor leisure space are shaded from excessive sunlight on the rear elevation by overhanging upper levels.

garden level
1 dining
2 kitchen
3 pantry
4 storage
5 ramp
6 play-room
7 veranda
8 swimming pool
9 garden

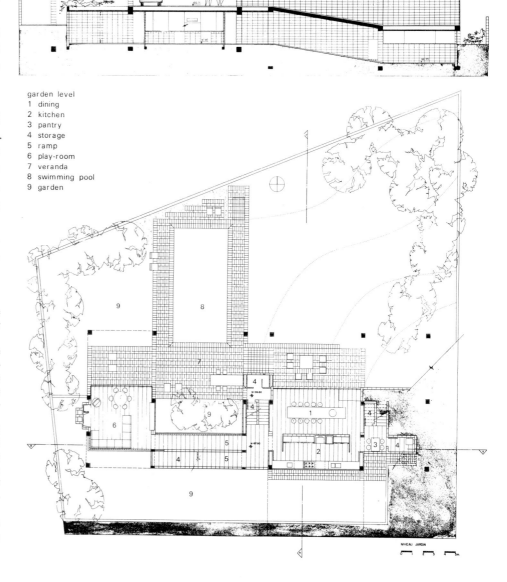

street level		upper level	
1 bridge	6 veranda	1 study	6 boys' bedrooms
2 carport	7 WC	2 master bedroom	7 guestroom
3 hall	8 service entry	3 closet	8 gallery
4 ramp	9 laundry	4 bath room	9 maid's room
5 living	10 service yard	5 girl's bedrooms	10 void
	11 void		

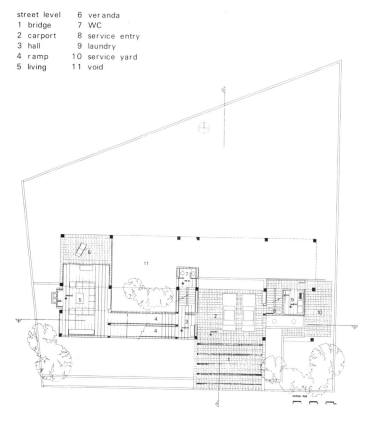

DEFINE RESIDENCE
São Paulo, 1978
Architect: Eduardo de Almeda

デファイネ邸

サンパウロ

設計：エドゥアルド・デ・アウメイダ

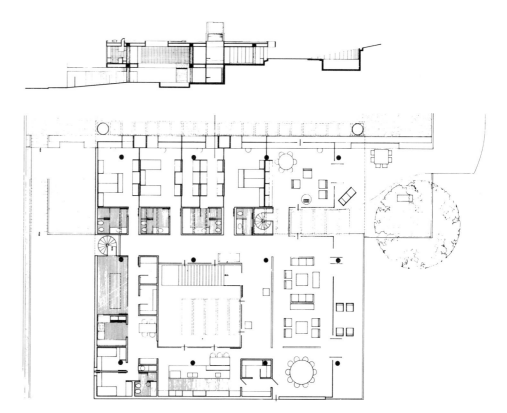

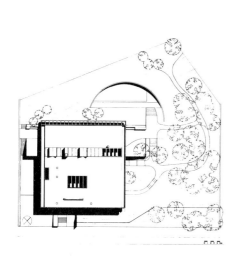

この住宅は都市の中にあるかなり広い不整形の敷地に建っており，以前その場所にあった建物の基礎を利用して設計されている．一組の夫婦と彼らのお客のために建てられたこの家は，部分的に地面から浮かされたプランとなった．

上部から光の入ってくる中庭として魅力を持つアトリウムの囲りに各部屋が配置されている．造園の処理とガラスを大々的に使用したことにより，内部空間と外部空間の視覚的，物理的な相互作用が高まっている．

コンクリート製の屋根スラブを使用したことにより，浴室上のトップライトや中庭上部に規則的な開口部を設けることが可能となった．

Situated on a large irregularly-shaped urban lot, this house is designed on the foundations of the previous house. Built for a couple and their guests, the program was solved in one partially elevated level.

Spaces are organized around a sky-lit atrium featured as a patio. Landscaping rend extensive use of glass accentuates the physical and visual indoor/outdoor interaction.

The concrete roof slab permits modular openings for skylights over the bathrooms and the patios.

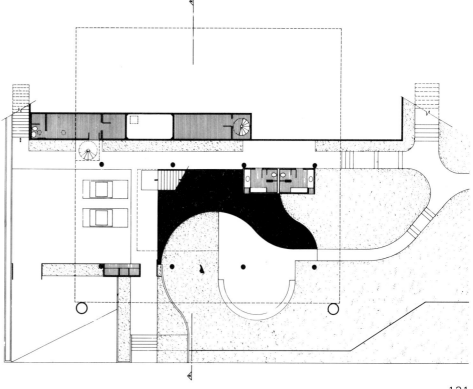

ANNEX FOR THE LEGISLATIVE ASSEMBLY
Curitiba, Paraná
Architect: Ramalho, Oba & Zamoner

下院議会別館

パラナ州クリチーバ

設計：ラマーリョ, オオバ＆ザモネール

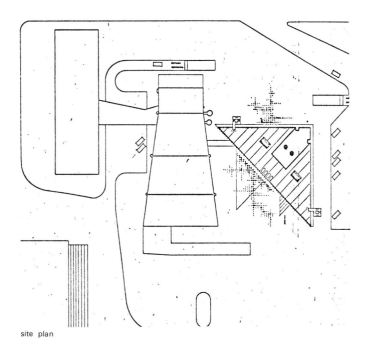

site plan

この計画は1976年に行われた設計競技で入選し，現在施工中である．建物は単純な線で構成され，統合された迫力を持ち，あいまいな都市景観の中でその機能を反映した造形的表現に満ちている．

視覚的な拡がりを残しつつ既存の建物群から適当な距離を保ち，かつ必要に応じて建物どうしを近づけなければならないという相反する二分法を解決するのに，カーテンウォールが役立った．部屋を線状に配置したことによって，そこを使用する人は明確な視界が確保され，直観的に動線を把握することができるのである．

この建物は空間的な豊かさを生み出していると同時に，理想的な建物の方向と自然な空気の対流制御によって質の高い調節可能な室内気候を創り出している．

This project, winner of a design competition in 1976, is now under construction. The project has simple lines, integrated vigor, and a plastic expression reflecting its function in the neutral urban scenery.

A curtain wall solves the dichotomy of necessary proximity and desirable distance from the existing surroundings while remaining visually open. The linear disposition of the rooms permits clear visualization and intuitive circulation by the users.

The building provides spatial enrichment and the creation of a controllable microclimate enhanced by its ideal orientation and natural air convention control.

1st floor

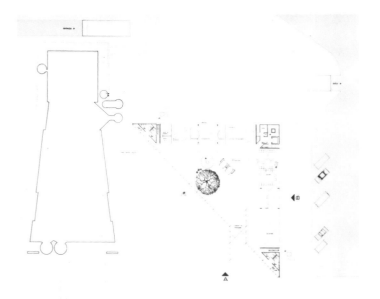

ground floor

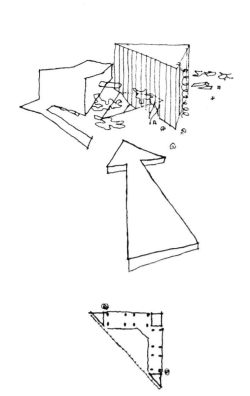
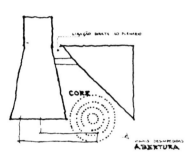
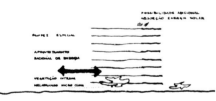
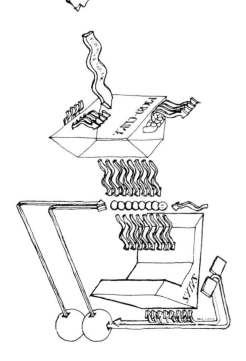

PERNAMBUCO EXPO CENTER

Recife, Pernambuco

Architect: Ramalho, Oba & Zamoner

ペルナンブーコ・エクスポ・センター

ペルナンブーコ州レシフェ

設計：ラマーリョ, オオバ＆ザモネール

この計画案は1977年に行われた設計競技で入選し，現在施工中である．近くのサウガジンニョという歴史的に重要な意味をもつ場所を，十分考慮に入れている．

造園は統合的な要素であり，それによって外部空間を組み立て，大きな建物の及ぼす影響を少なくしている．大面積の屋根でおおわれた空間であるにもかかわらず，視覚的には拡がりを残すことができるのもそのためである．この建築群の外部空間は穏やかに構成されているが，内部にはさまざまな雰囲気の空間が展開されている．

入場者は，8mのレベルにある中間階から入ると，建物全体を即座に見渡すことができる．歴史的に由緒ある敷地を保全するため，車のアプローチは裏側に設けられている．

構造は鉄骨とコンクリートでできている．電気，油圧，空調などを含む機械設備は3層目のレベルにある．換気と空気調和の機械システムは2重壁を垂直方向のダクトとして，また中空の梁を水平方向のダクトとして用いている．

This project won a design competition in 1977 and is now under construction. It takes into account the highly valued historical site of Salgadinho nearby.

The landscaping is an integrative element, organizing the exterior space, attenuating the effect of the mass and becoming a large covered space while remaining visually open. Serenely composed on the exterior, the complex houses a wide variety of interior atmospheres.

Entering on a mezzanine at the eight-meter level, the visitor visually perceives the whole building immediately. Respecting the integrity of the historical site, vehicular access is provided from the back.

The structure is physically both steel frame and reinforced concrete. Mechanical equipment, including electrical, hydraulic, and air-conditioning, is at the three-meter level. The mechanical system for air change and air conditioning uses double walls for vertical ducts and holes in beams for the horizontal.

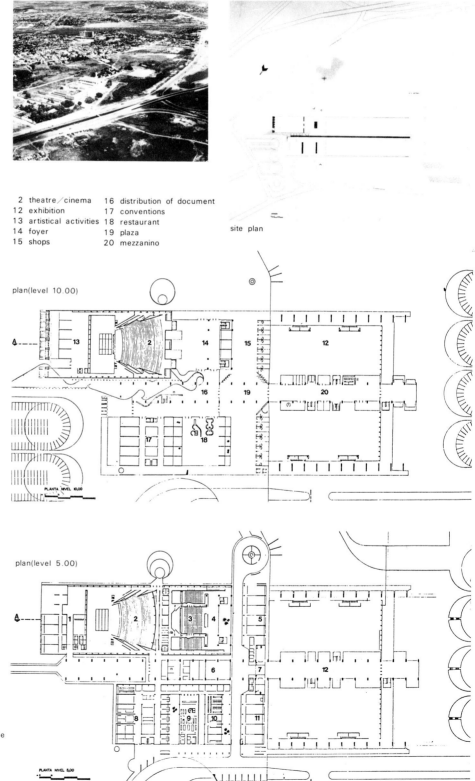

2 theatre/cinema
12 exhibition
13 artistical activities
14 foyer
15 shops
16 distribution of document
17 conventions
18 restaurant
19 plaza
20 mezzanino

site plan

plan(level 10.00)

plan(level 5.00)

1 side scene
2 theatre/cinema
3 convention
4 foyer
5 storage
6 facilities
7 administration
8 administration centre
9 kitchen
10 accomodation
11 workshop
12 exhibition

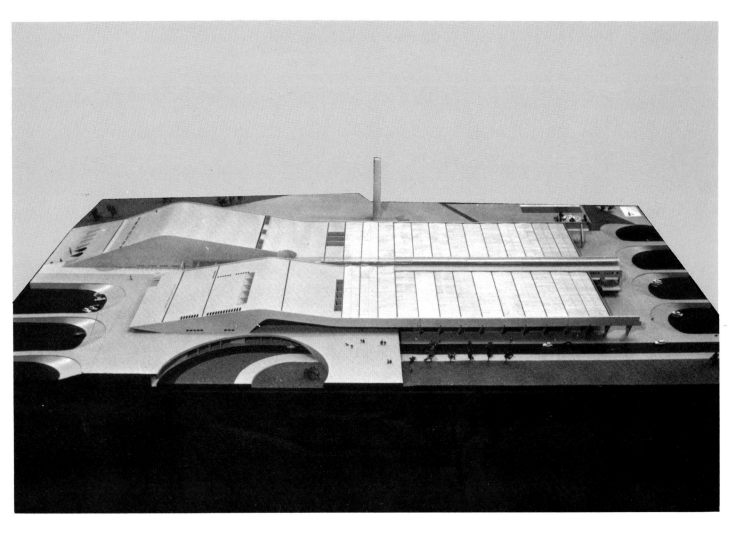

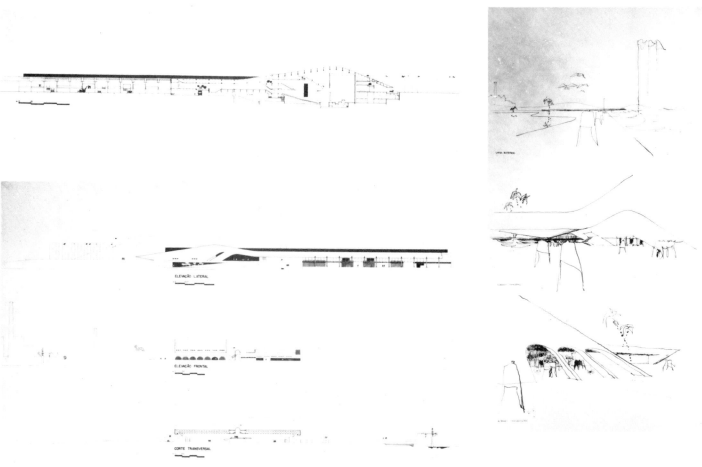

ELEVAÇÃO LATERAL

ELEVAÇÃO FRONTAL

CORTE TRANSVERSAL

TERRAFOTO HEADQUARTERS

Embu, São Paulo
Architect: Ramalho, Oba & Zamoner

テラフォト本社

サンパウロ州エンブー

設計：ラマーリョ，オオバ＆ザモネール

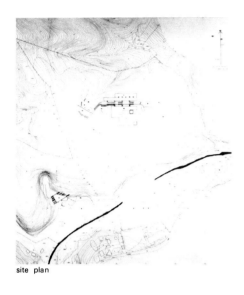
site plan

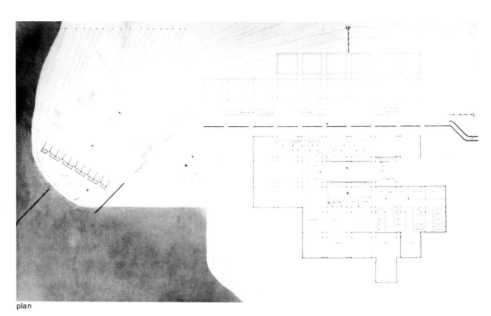
plan

航空調査会社の本社となるこの計画は，1979年に行われた設計競技の入選作である．計画を展開していく途中で，歴史的な土地であるエンブーに近いこの敷地の性格には当然関心が払われた．

仕事と余暇の生活空間を統合しようという目標の実現を第一に目ざした結果，建物は水平方向の動線を持つ平屋建てとなった．使用上，そして生活上必要なものと，保存し尊重していかねばならないものは常に対立関係にあるが，ここでは適切な空間構成によってそれをうまく解決している．

廊下部分は地形のうねりにそって曲折した軸を形づくっており，おもしろい視界を創り出している．エネルギーの合理的な使用法として太陽熱集熱器が備えられている．

elevation

This project, which will be the headquarters of an aerial survey company, won a competition for the design in 1979. Due respect was paid to the associations of the site, near historic Embu, in the development of the program.

As a consequence of the preoccupation with integrating the living space with job and leisure, the building is flat, making horizontal circulation obligatory. Appropriate spatial organization solves the eternal dichotomy between the necessity to use and dominate and that to preserve and respect.

The corridor forms a deflected spine, accomodating the ondulation of the topography and creating interesting perspectives. Solar collectors are provided as rational use of energy is a primary concern.

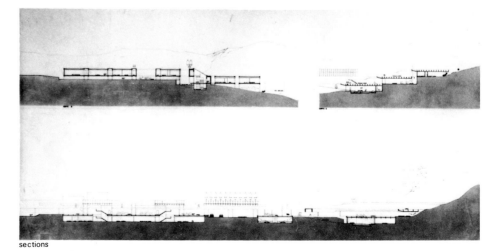
sections

140

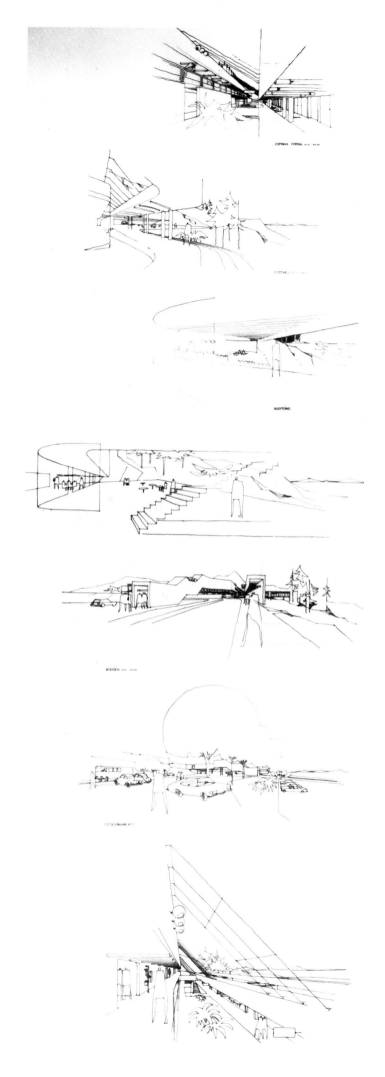

ACARPA HEADQUARTERS

Rua das Bandeiras, Curitiba, Paraná, 1977
Architect: Luiz Forte Neto

アカルパ本部
パラナ州クリチーバ市
設計：ルイス・フォルテ・ネット

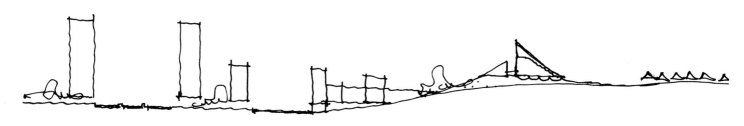

アカルパ (the Association for Credit and Rural Assistance of Parana) の本部は都市の中で密度が低いところから高くかわる部分に位置している。プログラムではこの密度の変化を考慮に入れて南側の立面をより高く，北側の立面は既存の市街地の水平線に調和するよう造形されている．
　水平の部材を用いて，年間を通しての太陽熱と光の理想的な調節を行っている．それゆえこの建物の特殊な形態は都市の中での配置の結果であり，また気候に対する適切な対応の結果である．そしてこれはアカルパの哲学を示している．アカルパは新しい技術的可能性を求めながら都市問題を大胆に追求することにその特徴がある．
　一つの連続した空間を生み出したこの建物は，異なった活動の分野間において，物理的にも心理的にもまた機能的にもそれらが統合される可能性を示している．基本的な設備と基幹施設を集中化したことによって，室内空間のレイアウトの変更が容易になっている．

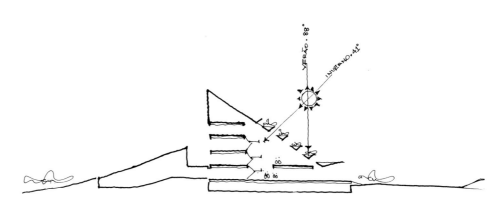

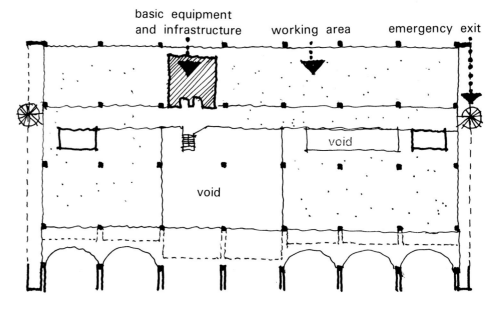

The headquarters of the Association for Credit and Rural Assistance of Paraná is located among urban areas of low and high density. The program takes into consideration the transition of densities, making the south facade higher and shaping the north facade to harmonize with the horizontal lines of the urban space.

Ideal control of sun and light throughout the year is obtained by the horizontal elements. The building's particular form, therefore, is the result of its urban setting, an appropriate response to the climate, and the philosophy of the institution it represents. ACARPA is characterized by a dynamic approach to rural problems, exploring new technical possibilities.

The solution of a single and continuous space permits the physical, psychological and functional integration of the different sectors of activities. The concentration of basic equipment and infrastructure permits flexibility in changing the interior space lay-out.

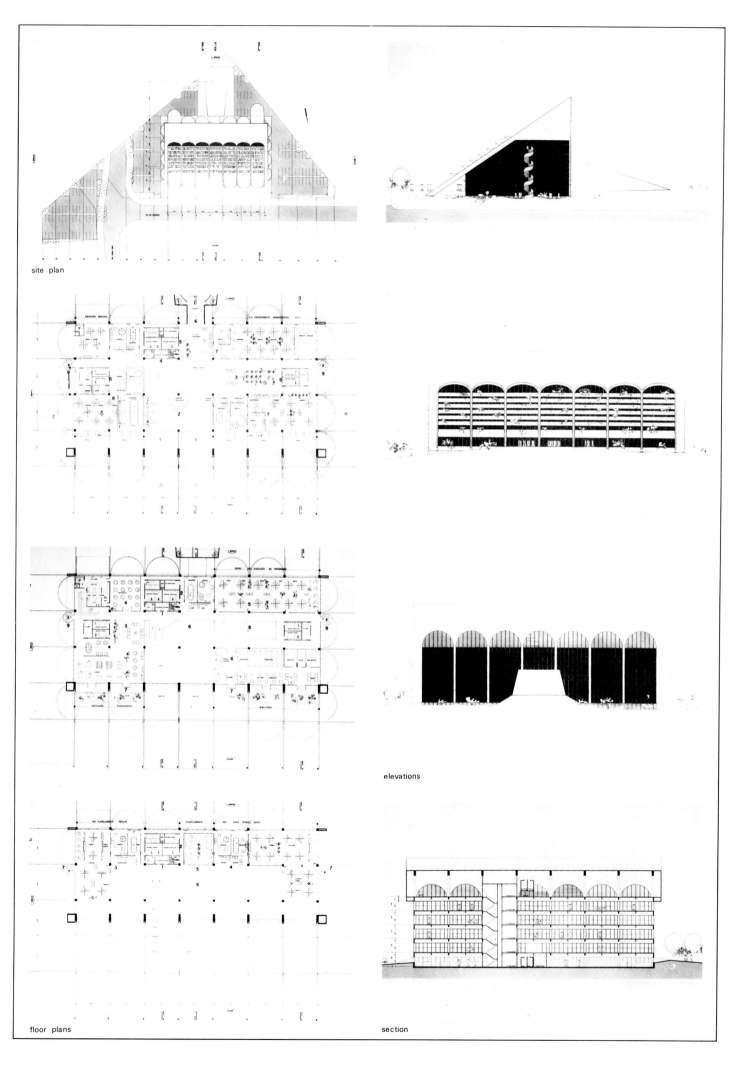

site plan

floor plans

elevations

section

ERPLAN HEADQUARTERS
Ribeirão Prêto, São Paulo
Architect: Lima, Machado, Matsuzawa & Yamaki

エルプラン本部

サンパウロ州リベイロン・プレット

設計：リーマ，マシャード，マツザワ＆ヤマキ

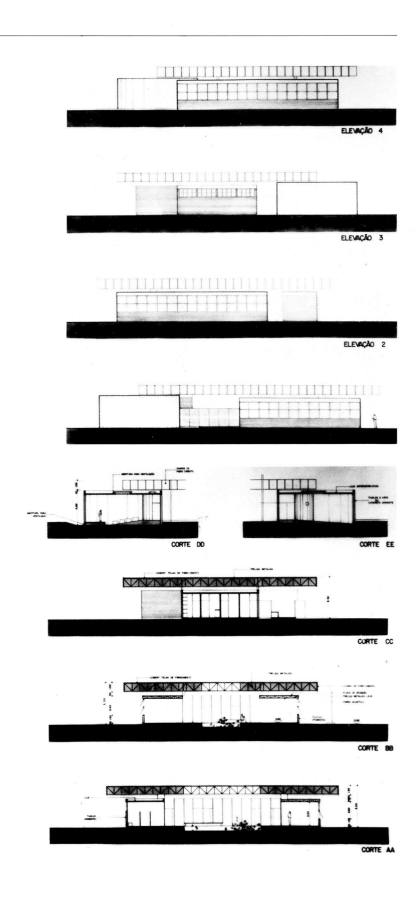

この計画は，地域計画省企画局の地方事務所であり，1976年に行われた設計競技で入選した．

建物の考え方は，空間的にもまた実体的にも中心の広場を核として構成されている．この建物は鉄骨造であり，短期間にかつ簡単に建設されたが，その印象は清潔で明解かつ単純である．

快適な室内温度と音響的快適さをますため，またゾーンごとの換気ができるよう，2重天井システムが採用されている．室内空間は理想的な自由度を持つ可動間仕切で区切られている．

広場を創ることによって建物それ自体の存在感が最少限にとどめられる一方，人間どうしのつきあいは容易になるということが意図されている．中庭はそこ独自の気候をつくり出しており，人間のためのものであることを強調している．

This is a project for a Regional Office of the Secretary of Planning; it won a design competition in 1976.

The concept is of a building spatially and physically organized around a central plaza. Sheltered by a metal frame structure quickly and easily constructed, the building is clear, defined and simple.

A double ceiling system is adopted to aid thermal and acoustic comfort and to permit zonal ventilation. Interior spaces are defined by movable partitions, achieving an ideal degree of flexibility.

The creation of a common plaza is intended to minimize the presence of the building itself and to facilitate human relations. The inner garden creates a micro-climate, emphasizing the orientation toward people.

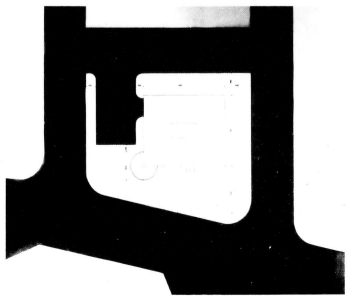
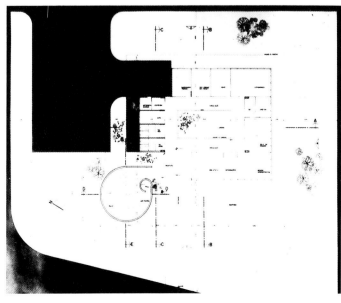

BRAZIL——KALEIDOSCOPE OF ARCHITECTURE

by K. Narumi + H. Yamaki

ブラジル──建築のカレイドスコープ

鳴海邦碩＋ウンベルト八巻

コーヒーとサンバの国ブラジル．建築家にとっては，ニーマイヤーとブラジリアのブラジルということになろうか．人々がある国を思いうかべるとき，そのイメージは，ともすれば単純な要素に固定されがちである．それは，フジヤマとゲイシャの国日本，あるいは，丹下と銀座の日本，と同じ認識パターンである．

現実のブラジルは，国土面積において日本の約24倍，人口１億1000万人の大国であり，その国土は実に多様な生活空間から構成されている．この多様さは，バラエティーに富んだ風土と，人種のるつぼともいわれる人種構成によってもたらされたものである．

ブラジルの原住民はインディオ であるが，1500年，アルヴァレス・カブラルがこの大陸を発見して以来，ポルトガル人と黒人が新住人として加わることになった．ブラジルの主な住人が，インディオ，黒人，ポルトガル人であった期間は，300 年以上続くことになったが，この間に，これら３系統の文化を基底とするブラジル文化ともいうべきものが醸成されたのである．

1888年の奴隷制度の廃止に相前後して，ヨーロッパやアジアから多数の移民が導入されることになった．このため，ブラジルの人種構成は一段と複雑になったのである．ある人類学者の報告によると，ブラジルには，20数種類の皮膚

の色を表わす言葉があるといわれるが，この人種構成の多様さを思えばなるほどとうなずける．

ブラジルの国土は広大であると同時に，熱帯から，乾燥地帯，温帯などにいたる，様々な地域によって構成される．この広大さのためもあり，まだまだ未開の地は多い．大都市，中小都市，農山村によって構成される地域構造は，どの国にも見い出すことができるが，ブラジルでは，海岸から内陸にいたる距離は，キロメートルで測るべきではなく，時代で計るべきだといわれている．文明化の度合の異なった地域によって構成されているというのである．

人種的に多種多様な国民，バラエティーに豊

For most of us Brazil is the land of coffee and samba; for architects, perhaps, the land of Oscar Niemeyer and Brasilia. Our impressions of foreign countries consist of very simple images, just as Japan is known abroad for Fujiyama and geisha, or Kenzo Tange and the Ginza.

Brazil covers an area roughly 24 times that of Japan, with a population of 110 million and diverse ways of life. This variety stems from its range of climates and its collection of peoples; the country is a veritable racial melting pot.

The original Brazilian natives are, of course, the Indians. In 1500, the conti-

nent was discovered by Pedro Alvares Cabral of Portugal, and many Portugese and blacks came after him to the country. The population has consisted mainly of Indians, blacks, and Portugese for over 300 years, and the cultures of the three groups have melded to form a distinctly Brazilian culture.

Around the time of the abolition of slavery in 1888, various Europeans and Asians found their way to Brazil, and the composition of Brazil's population became even more complex. Anthropologists tell us there are some 20 different words to describe skin color in the langu-

age, a fact that is easy to understand when Brazil's racial make-up is considered.

Brazil is huge and includes tropical, arid, and humid regions among others. The land is so big that some areas are still undeveloped. The different regions of any country have their large cities, towns, and rural settlements, but in Brazil's case, distance from the coast inland is measured in ages, not kilometers. The country is composed of different regions with differing degrees of civilization. Its people have a variety of backgrounds and of lifestyles, and its architecture, too, offers a

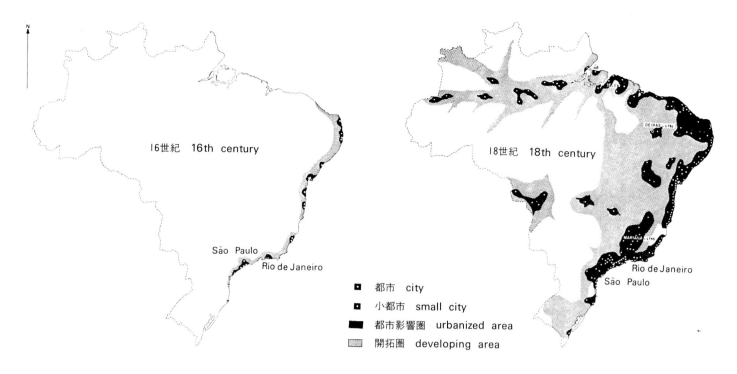

① ブラジルにおける開発と都市化の進行. Ref.3　The development and progress of urbanization in Brazil. Ref. 3

んだ生活空間．そしてまた，ブラジルは建築においても，万華鏡の世界を見せてくれるのである．

ポルトガル植民都市とスペイン植民都市

ブラジルの開発は，当然のことながら，まず沿岸部から進められた．沿岸部を南下し，そして内陸部に進展していく各時代の開発状況が①に示されている．

ポルトガル人の植民が開始されたのは，1532年，最初の植民者400名が現在のサントス港近くに上陸し，サトウキビの栽培を始めたときからのことである．1582年には，ペルナンブーコが製糖工場数66，人口4000人，バイーアが工場数36，人口15000人の都市に発展していたのである．当時の都市としては，この他に，リオデジャネイロとサンパウロがあった．

当時のバイーアの都市図②をみると，ヨーロッパの中世都市のように城壁で囲まれ，聖堂を核とする構成となっている．街路や広場の構成パターンには，規則性をみることはできない．この不規則性は，歴史的建造物が数多く残存し今や観光地となっているオーロ・プレットにおいても同様である．

これに対し，スペイン植民都市は，カラカスの都市図を見てもわかるように，整然とした碁盤目状となっている③．これは，リマ，ブエノスアイレスをはじめ，メンドサやラ・パスなど，スペイン植民都市に共通したパターンである．スペイン王が，新大陸における新都市建設にあたって守るべき基準を定めたためである．この形態はどうも，ローマの植民都市が下敷きとなっているらしい．

スペイン人は，中央集権的な行政制度を植民地に移植し，スペイン王はその制度を通じて植民地を支配した．新世界における都市は植民地統治のための重要な機関として建設されたのである．

ところが，ポルトガル人の植民地においては，

kaleidoscopic variety.

Portugese and Spanish Colonial Cities

The development of Brazil began along the coast, moving south and then inland, as shown in ①. The first to arrive were 400 Portuguese colonists, who landed near what is now Santos Bay in 1532. By 1582 Pernambuco had 66 sugar refineries with a population of 4,000 and Bahia had 36 refineries with 15,000 inhabitants. Other cities of that time were Rio de Janeiro and Sao Paulo.

A contemporary map of Bahia ② shows a form similar to that of medieval European cities, enclosed by a wall with a church at its core. Its streets and plazas adhere to no pattern at all. Ouro Prêto is a similar city, with no rational plan and with many old buildings remaining.

The Spanish colonists, on the other hand, built cities to a definite order, as in Caracas ③. The same pattern is seen in other Spanish colonial cities such as Lima, Buenos Aires, Mendoza and La Paz. The King of Spain felt that a certain basic order should be maintained in the construction of new cities on the new continent; that order is apparently based on the colonial cities of old Rome.

The Spanish brought with them the centralized system of authority by which their king ruled his colonies. Their cities were built as important instruments of his rule in the New World.

The Portugese, on the other hand, brought with them the big landowner system with its emphasis on the plantation. Their cities were founded as tentative housing for those who had just arrived and were never accorded the importance which the Spanish attached to their cities.

The housing of Brazil's colonial era bears a spatial resemblance to Japan's

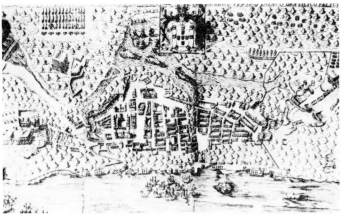

② 17世紀バイーアの都市図. Ref. 4　Bahia. Seventeenth-century Plan. Ref. 4

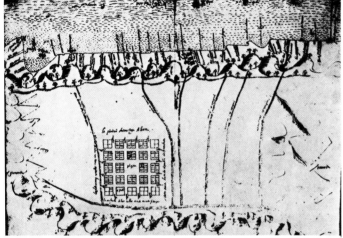

③ 16世紀カラカスの都市図. Ref. 6　Caracas. Sixteenth-century Plan. Ref. 6

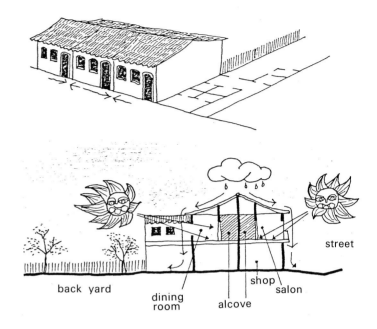

④ ポルトガル植民都市の都市住宅. Ref. 5
Urban housing of a Portugese colonial city. Ref. 5

当初から大土地所有制がとり入れられ，プランテーションが諸活動の中心であった．都市は本国からやってきたばかりのポルトガル人の一時的な居住地として位置づけられていたのであり，都市は，スペイン植民地におけるほど重要視されていなかったのである．

ブラジル植民期の都市住宅は，日本の伝統的な都市住宅である「まちや」に類似した空間構成をもっていた．敷地の形状は，間口10メートル程度の短冊状であり，建物は道路に沿って平入りの形式でつくられ，隣の建物とは，ほぼ同じ高さで接して建てられた．このような形式は，中世ルネッサンス期のポルトガルにおける伝統的な都市住宅の形式そのままであるといわれている④．こうしたブラジルの伝統的都市住宅は，今日でも，ポルトガル植民の基地となった沿岸都市や内陸部の小都市には今なお多数存在している．また，サンパウロなどの大都市においても，旧市街にその存続をみい出すことができる⑦⑩⑪．

スペイン植民都市ではパティオ型の住宅が一般的である．これは前述の新都市建設の布告のなかの次のような規定が強く作用しているためと考えられる――「外からの攻撃にそなえ建物は独立させず連なっていること．馬をつなぎ，動物を飼うため，また衛生や健康のためできるだけ広いパティオをもつこと」．

ポルトガル植民都市の都市住宅は，街路または広場に対して直接開かれた構造をとるのに対し，スペイン植民都市のそれでは，街路はなかば閉じられたパティオの空間に結びつき，住居は街路に対して閉じられた構造をとるのである．

複合した伝統と建築

ブラジルの基底的な文化は，インディオ，黒人，ポルトガル人の3つの文化系統の混淆によってもたらされたものであるといわれる．しかし，ブラジルの文化はこれだけに限られるわけではない．前世紀のなかば以降，ヨーロッパやアジ

traditional *machiya*, an urban housing form.

The site itself is a narrow strip with the short dimension, about ten meters, facing the road. The hip of the simple roof runs parallel to the road. The houses are built contiguous to, and at nearly the same height as, each other. This is the very form of traditional urban housing in medieval and Renaissance Portugal④. Much of this traditional Brazilian housing remains today in the coastal cities and inland towns of the old Portuguese colonists. Parts of the old cities are still to be found in cities like São Paulo⑦⑩⑪.

The patio house is common in Spanish colonial cities. This form was prescribed by decree in the construction of new cities, as mentioned above: "In anticipation of attack from outside, houses are to be connected and not independent. They are to include patios as large as possible to permit typing of horses and domestic animals and for the sake of sanitation and health."

While homes in Portugese colonial cities opened directly onto the town's streets and plazas, in Spanish colonial cities, housing was closed to the street and opened instead to the patio.

Composite Traditions and Architecture

Brazilian culture is often described as a jumble of Indian, black, and Portugese cultures, but in reality it is not limited to just these. Immigrants from all over Europe and Asia have been arriving since the middle of the last century and the influence of their cultures is widely felt⑤.

The front line areas of immigrant settlement were governed almost independently. Until transportation and methods of communication made their remarkable progress, such immigrant settlements remained closed societies.

The Japanese cities of the state of

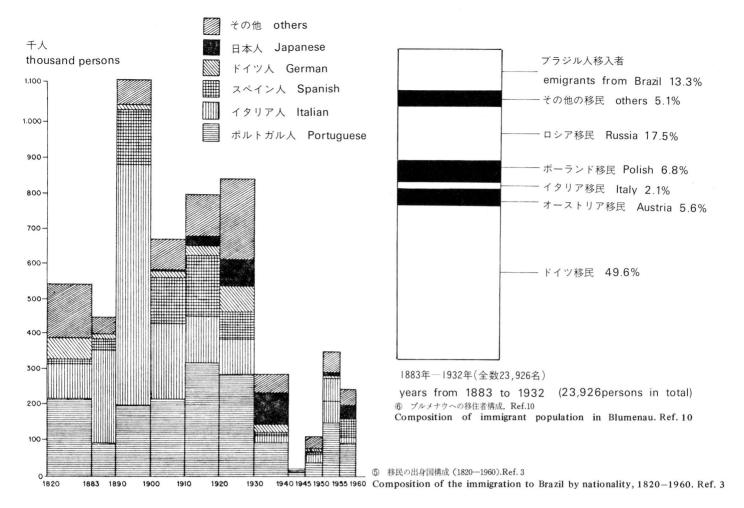

⑤ 移民の出身国構成（1820—1960）. Ref. 3
Composition of the immigration to Brazil by nationality, 1820–1960. Ref. 3

⑥ ブルメナウへの移住者構成. Ref. 10
Composition of immigrant population in Blumenau. Ref. 10

アから多数の移民が導入されたが，こうした人人がもたらした文化の影響もまた大きい⑤．

こうした外国移民の移住地は，開拓前戦にほとんど孤立して営まれた．交通やコミュニケーション手段が著しい進歩をみせるまでの間，閉鎖的な移住社会が形成されていたのである．

パラナ州北部の日系移民都市，サンタ・カタリナ州のドイツ系移民都市，リオ・グランデ・ド・スル州のイタリア系移民都市などが，この例である．これらの都市はいわば純粋培養的に形成された履歴をもち，そこでは今日でも，本国そのままの建築様式が維持されていたり，生活慣習がまもられていたりする．

サンタ・カタリナ州ブルメナウは，現在人口10万人余りの地域中心都市であるが，ブルメナウ博士を中心としたドイツ移民によって開発された都市である．この地域にはひき続いて，オーストリア，ポーランド，北イタリアなどからの移民も入植することとなったが，全体としてみても北ヨーロッパからの住民が大半を占める⑥．

この地域には，エンシャイメールと呼ばれる木骨住宅が多く，これはこの地域の建築の特色とされている．この構法は，材木で構造体をつくり，すき間にレンガをつめたものである⑧⑨．これには，ドイツ本国のバイエルン地方の住宅に類似した表情がうかがわれるのである⑫．

この地域の多くの建物は，急勾配の屋根をもつ．これは，北ヨーロッパにこそ必要であるが，雪のないこのブルメナウの地では不要のものである．室内の家具，調度や，バルコニーや窓辺の花など，ドイツ南部地域の住宅を連想させる．

近年このブルメナウでは，伝統的な様式で建築物を建てることが奨励されている．一定期間の不動産税の免除などの特典があるのだ．この地域には，ドイツを中心とする北ヨーロッパからの移民が多いといっても，これらに共通した一定の建築様式があるわけではない．しかし，最近つくられている建物をみると，ドイツのバイエルン地方やオーストリアのチロル地方のロ

Paraná, the German cities of Santa Catarina and the Italian cities of Rio Grande do Sul are examples of such societies. The history of these cities is one of development in relative isolation and even today the building styles and daily customs of their respective homelands are maintained.

Blumenau, in the state of Santa Catarina, is a regional center with a population of over 100,000, and was founded by German settlers led by Dr. Blumenau. Austrians, Poles, and northern Italians followed to this region, and all together northern Europeans account for over one-half of the immigrants to the area ⑥.

The region is noted for its wood-frame houses, called *enxaimel*. The frame is erected of timbers which are left exposed to view, and the walls infilled with brick ⑧ ⑨. The resulting expression resembles that of homes of the Bayern district of Germany ⑫.

Most of the buildings in this area have roofs of steep slope; this is necessary in northern Europe but not in Blumenau, which never gets any snow. The furniture and fixtures, balconies and flowers in the windows of buildings here also recall those of south Germany.

Blumenau has recently been encouraging building in the traditional style with exemptions from real estate tax for fixed periods and other incentives. But, although most immigration to the area came from north Europe and especially Germany, all groups do not share the same building style. However, most new buildings seem to aim at the picturesque styles of the Bayern region of Germany and the Tirol of Austria. Efforts are being made to present a new traditional form based on a homogenous image. This may be seen as another Brazilian assimilation of the old Continental cultures ⑬ ⑭.

⑦ 小都市ポソ・デ・フォラ（バイーア州）の伝統的住宅.
⑧ ブルメナウ近郊，エンシャイメールの住宅.
⑨ ジョインビレの北ヨーロッパ風の住宅.
⑩ オーロ・プレットの都市住宅.
⑪ フロリアノポリスの都市住宅.

⑦ Indigenous Housing in Pau de Fora.
Photo: J. Guedes.
⑧ Enxaimel style housing in Blumenau area.
⑨ North European-style housing in Joinville.
⑩ Urban housing in Ouro Preto.
Photo: C. Matsuzawa.
⑪ Urban housing in Florianopolis.
Photos ⑧ ⑨ ⑪ : *K. Narumi.*

マンチックな建築様式が志向されているらしい．こうした共有可能なイメージに基づいて，新しい伝統的建築形態を造り出していこうというのである．これもまた，旧大陸文化のブラジル化のひとつのかたちであると思われる⑬⑭．

多様な風土と建築

狩猟と焼畑農業で生活するアマゾンのインディオにとって，住居は一時的なシェルターにすぎない．獲物や新しい栽培地を求めて移動しなくてはならないから，それにあわせて住居を移動させる必要がある．また，草ぶきの屋根は1，2年もすると，虫の巣になってしまうので，焼き払って別の場所に新しい住居をつくることにもなる．

熱帯地方では，草の住居は窓はないが通風がよく，内部は意外に涼しい．夜間は多少冷え込むので，家の中の炉ではいつも火がたかれている．これはまた虫よけの働きもする．

こうしたインディオの住居形態は，アマゾン地域の一般のブラジル人たちの住居にもとり入れられている．風土に適合した住居形態なのだ．

アマゾン地域の入口ともいえるところ，アマゾン横断道路沿いにマラバという町がある．この町の周辺の集落の住居は草ぶきのロングハウス様の形態をもつが，インディオの住居と原理的にはかわることがない．

Y字型の自然木を掘っ立てで建て，この間に棟木をわたす．これに切妻式にババスーの葉（この地方に多いヤシの一種で，この葉にはワックス分が含まれている）で屋根をふく．壁も同じく，ババスーでつくられるが，場合によっては地上1.7から2メートルあたりまで土壁とすることもある．

ババスーは100枚単位で採取人から購入するのだが，これを使って1日で家が建ってしまう．家を棟続きで継ぎたしていくと，材料も手間もはぶける．これで，平入りのロングハウスのような住居群構成ができあがっていくのである．

Various Climes and Architecture

The homes of the hunting and burn-farming Amazonian Indians is nothing more than temporary shelter. Their housing must meet their need to move to find game and new arable land. After one or two years, thatched roofs become home to too many insects, are burned and new homes built somewhere else.

* Grass houses of the tropics have no windows but ventilation is good and the interiors are unexpectedly cool. Nights can be chilly, so a fire is kept burning in the hearth. This also helps to discourage insects. This indigenous form of housing has been adapted by most Brazilians in the Amazon region; it is a form of housing best suited to the climate.

The town of Marabá is on the highway which crosses the Amazon. There and in other settlements nearby are grass-thatched long houses, but these are not, as a rule, Indian homes. Trees of a natural Y-shape are sunk in the ground and beams laid across them. The hipped roofs are thatched with Babaçú leaves, which have a waxy finish and are abundant in the area. The walls are similarly thatched with Babaçú but in some cases mud walls up to 1.7 meters or two meters in height are found.

Thatched walls promote good ventilation and are most suitable to this tropical region, and the waxy Babaçú also help repel water.

Interiors have two rooms, one for daily activities and one for sleeping. Cooking is done in a corner of the living area. Sometimes the sleeping area is divided into two rooms by a plaited screen of Babaçú hung between them. Partitions of Babaçú, however, provide no privacy, yet the region's residents boast of their wide-open lifestyle ⑮ ⑯.

⑩

⑪

⑫ ドイツ，バイエルン地方の農家．Ref.12
⑬⑭ ブルメナウで推奨されている建築デザイン．
⑮⑯ マラバの草葺きの家．

⑫ German homestead in the Bayern district. Ref. 12
⑬⑭ The architectural design currently recommended in Blumenau. *Photo: K. Narumi.*
⑮⑯ Thatched houses at Maraba, northern Brazil. *Photo: H. Yamaki.*

ババスーの壁は風通しがいいので，この熱帯性の地域では，快適な居住環境が得られる．また，葉にふくまれるワックス分が，防水の役割を果たしてくれる．

部屋は居間と寝室の二つからなり，炊事は居間の片すみで行われる．寝室を2室に分割することもあるが，この場合には，ババスーで編んだムシロをつるす．ババスーの壁やパーティションではプライバシーもなにもあったものではない．しかし，この地域の人々は，開けっ広げな家庭生活を自慢にさえするのである⑮⑯．

アマゾン地域の中心都市であるマナーウスには，ゴムブーム時代にイタリアから運んだ大理石でつくられた劇場がある．

近年モダン建築の建設も多い．しかし，インディオ式の草の家が，これからも庶民の住宅として利用され続けるだろうことは，まずまちがいあるまい．

モダニズムとコロニアル・スタイル趣味

ブラジリアは，近代都市計画と近代建築の一大成果である．行政官庁の建物も，集合住宅も，いわゆる現代建築そのものである．特に大使館地区においては，それぞれの国が現代建築の妍を競っている．

ブラジリアの中心市街地内に，私が知っている限りでは唯一の，非モダニズム建築がある．それは，本派本願寺の建物である．近くには，ステンドグラスで有名な聖ジョアン・ボスコ教会があり，この一帯を宗教施設地区にしようという計画があるとも聞く．ともかく，この和風建築は，近代建築で構成されたブラジリアの都市空間にみる，ちょっとしたきまぐれである⑳．

ブラジリアには，市街地の東部に広大な人工湖がつくられており，その周辺地区は高級住宅地となっている．この住宅地は，まさに大邸宅地区とも呼ばれるべき地区で，閣僚など高級官僚達が多く住んでいる．ここの住宅の大半は，白い壁と茶色の瓦がのった反り屋根をもつコロ

In the Amazon's central city of Manaus is a theater built of Italian marble in the era of the rubber boom. There is also a deal of modern architecture there, but the native grass house will surely continue to be employed as housing for the greater number of the area's inhabitants.

Modernism and the Colonial Styles

Brasilia is a product of modern city planning and modern architecture. The administrative buildings and housing blocks are modern architecture itself. Especially in the consular section, each country is competing in the language of architecture.

I know of only one building in downtown Brasilia which is not Modern and that is the Honpa Honganji Temple ⑳. The famous stained glass church of São João Bosco is nearby; there is talk of a plan to make this Brasilia's religious center. Still, this Japanese-style building looks whimsical amidst its neighbors ⑲.

On the eastern side of Brasilia is a man-made lake and the area around it is one of the city's best residential sections. Cabinet members and other bureaucrats live in the grand homes here, the majority of which have the white walls and brown-tiled roofs of the colonial style ⑰ ⑱.

The colonial style is the legacy of the Portugese colonists and in all regions the homes of those settlers are peserved. The style is that of the farm houses of northern Portugal. In those we can see today, the white walls are boldly contrasted by coal black openings, giving them an ascetic appearance. In contrast, the homes of Brasilia sport blue picture tiles on their white walls as ornament which serves to heighten the picturesque effect of surrounding flowers and trees.

This type of home is seen not only in Brasilia, but in the upper-class residential

ニアル・スタイルなのである⑰⑱．

このコロニアル・スタイルは，ポルトガル植民時代の開拓者住宅の伝統を受け継ぐもので，今でも各地にこうした開拓者住宅が保存されている⑲．これは，ポルトガル本国の北部地域の農家の様式であるといわれている．

今日わたしたちがみることのできる，植民時代の開拓者住宅は，白い壁とそこに開けられた黒々とした開口部がくっきりとした対比をみせ，禁欲的なイメージをかもしだしている．これに対し，ブラジリアの邸宅は，白い壁面に青いタイル画がはめこまれたり，装飾に工夫がこらされている．周囲に配された花や樹木が，より一層絵葉書的効果を高めている．

この種の邸宅は，ブラジリアのみでなく，サンパウロの高級住宅地にも数多く見ることができる．植民時代の開拓者の住居が，コロニアル・スタイルとして，今や特権階級の人々のものとなったのである．

特権階級の人々のうちどの程度がポルトガル系市民であるかは不明であるが，そうした系を問わずとも，コロニアル・スタイル趣味は一般的な傾向とみてよいであろう．彼等の住居形態に対する最終的願望が，いわゆるモダニズム建築にあるのではなく，こうしたコロニアル・スタイルにあるということは，ひとつの伝統志向のあらわれとみることができよう．

ブラジルの国民の人種構成と地域空間の多様性からときおこし，ブラジルのヴァナキュラーな建築についての素描を試みた．このなかでひとつ興味をひくのは，建築形態における伝統志向の存在である．

ブラジリアの特権階級の住居がコロニアル・スタイルをとることは，バンディランテ（奥地開拓者）の子孫であるという，彼等のアイデンティティの象徴であるのかもしれない．このことはまた，ドイツ系移民都市の新伝統形成志向ともつながるものである．モダニズム建築が花

sections of São Paulo as well. The style of the colonial settlers is now that of the current priviledged class. Though it isn't known to what extent the descendents of the original colonists live in such homes, the colonial style itself has become simply a general trend in taste. The ultimate aspiration in building styles there is not Modern, but Colonial, reflecting traditional hopes and aims.

Conclusion

This has been a rough sketch of Brazil's vernacular architecture, with her many peoples and various climates. One of the most interesting observations is the existence of traditional preferences in architectural form.

The fact that the priviledged class of Brasilia has adopted the Colonial style may be meant to identify the members of that class as descendents of the *bandeirante,* the original settlers. This is the idea behind the new traditional forms in the cities of the German settlers. That Modernism should flourish alongside architecture of more traditional intentions is by no means limited to Brazil. However, something basic to Brazilian culture may be found in what the Brazilians themselves are trying to find in their traditions.

As mentioned elsewhere, the Niemeyer style continues to be the mainstream in current Brazilian architecture. It is unheard of in other countries for the strength of influence of one architect to be so long sustained. Even Japan's passion for Le Corbusier does not approach this.

Just as the Colonial tastes of Brazil's priviledged classes and the Bayern and Tirolian styles of her north European descendents are expressions of Brazilian tradition.

⑰

⑱

⑰⑱ コロニアル・スタイルの邸宅.
⑲ 16世紀の開拓者の家. サンパウロ州コチア. Ref. 9
⑳ ブラジリアの本派本願寺.

⑰⑱ Residences in Colonial style.
Photo: K. Narumi.
⑲ A house of the early colonial period. Ref. 9
⑳ The Honpa Honganji temple in Brasilia.
Photo: K. Narumi.

を咲かせていると同時に，一方でこうした伝統志向がうかがえるのは，なにもブラジルに限ったことではない．しかしブラジルの人々がなにに伝統を見い出そうとしているかをみることによって，彼等の文化的基盤をさぐり出すことができるのではないかと思われるのである．

他稿で述べられているように，ブラジルの現代建築においては，ニーマイヤー・スタイルがあいかわらず主流を占めている．他の国では，一人の建築家の影響がこれほど強力に持続することは考えられない．日本におけるコルビュジエ趣味にしても，これ程強烈ではない．

ブラジルにおける特権階級のコロニアル・スタイル趣味や北ヨーロッパ系ブラジル人のバイエルン型，チロル型建築趣味が，ひとつのブラジル的伝統志向の表われではないかと考えるわけであるが，ニーマイヤー趣味もまた，ひとつの伝統志向であるとするのは強引にすぎるであろうか．

参考文献　References

1 斉藤広志『新しいブラジル』
Hiroshi Saito "New Brazil".

2 斉藤広志，中川文雄共著『ラテンアメリカ現代史Ⅰ』
H. Saito, Fumio Nakagawa, "Modern History of Latin America I"

3 A. Azevedo, "Brazil a terra e o homen Vol. II".

4 Nestor G. R. Filho, "Evolução Urbana do Brazil".

5 Nestor G. R. Filho, "Quadro da Arquitetura no Brazil."

6 E. Y. Galantay, "New Towns: Antiquity to the Present".

7 W. D. Harris Jr., "The Growth of Latin American Cities".

8 J. D. Mesa, T. Gisbert La Paz eu el siglo XVIII, "Boletin del Centro de Investigaciones Historicas y Esteticas, Facultad de Arquitectura y Urbanismo, Universidad Central de Venezuela, No. 20".

9 "Atlas dos Monumentos Históricos e Artísticos do Brasil".

10 Relatório do Campus Avançado da USP 46 a equipe.

11 "Centenário de Blumenau".

12 T. Gebhard, "Der Bauernhof in Bayern".

鳴海邦碩：大阪大学助教授，都市計画家
Kunihiro Narumi : Associate Professor of Osaka University
ウンベルト八巻：建築家
HUMBERTO YAMAKI : ARCHITECT

DATA 作品データ
CREDITS 作品クレジット
BIOGRAPHIES 設計者略歴

CARVALHAL RESIDENCE
Location: Ponta do Parurú, Ibiúna, São Paulo, 1977
Assistant: Chico Baffa, Paulo Del Nero
Consultant: Mariano Mairal Argental (Structural), José Maria de Castro Ferreira (Hydraulic), Alfredo Akira Ohnuma (Electrical)
Constructor: Mestre Oreste Caputo

*

ABREU RESIDENCE
Location: Fazenda Veneza, Valinhos, São Paulo, 1976
Assistant: Marilia Penteado Sant Anna de Almeida, Valeria Wey, Manoel Geraldo Cação Pereira
Consultant: Tedeschi & Ogata (Structural), ETIP (Mechanical)
Constructor: CEMPLA

*

ITORORO VILLAGE URBAN RENOVATION
Location: Bela Vista, São Paulo, 1976
Architect: Decio Tozzi, Benedito Lima de Toledo, Claudio Tozzi
Assistant: Laudelino de Carvalho Neto, Milton Esteves Junior, Odair Carlos de Almeida
Consultant: Aracy Amaral (Cultural Destination), Roberto Burle Marx (Landscape), Julio Abe Wakahara (Survey), Claudio Tozzi, Julio Abe Wakahara (Visual Communication), Luiz Antonio V. Keating (Drafting)

Architect

Decio Tozzi
Born in São Paulo, 1936. Graduated from the School of Architecture, Mackenzie University, 1960.

デーシオ・トッズィ
1936年サンパウロに生まれる。1960年マッケンジー大学建築科卒業。

CAMPOS DO JORDÃO TELEPHONE EXCHANGE
Location: Abernéssia, Campos do Jordão, São Paulo, 1973
Collaborator: Helio Pasta, Helio Penteado, Julio Katinsky, Alfred Talaat
Consultant: Shiguer Mitsutani (Structure), J. Paolone (Mechanical)
Constructor: Construtora Iter

*

IBIUNA TELEPHONE EXCHANGE
Location: Ibiuna, São Paulo, 1974
Collaborator: Helio Pasta, Helio Penteado, Julio Katinsky, José Ricardo Carvalho
Consultant: José Parisi (Structural), PROMON Engenharia (Mecanical)
Constructor: Sistema Arquitetura e Construção

*

BANESPA BUTANTÃ BANK
Location: Butantã, São Paulo, 1976
Collaborator: Alfred Talaat, Takeshi Katsumata
Consultant: Shiguer Mitsutani, Guentaro Kimura, Engetherm
Constructor: Constructora GTO

*

CETESB LABORATORY
Location: São Paulo, 1976
Collaborator: José Maria Whitaker de Assumpção, Takeshi Katsumata
Consultant: Mario Frenco (Structural), Engetherm
Constructor: INTARCO

Architect

Ruy Ohtake, Arquitetura e Urbanismo S/C LTDA
Established in 1962.
Ruy Ohtake
Born in São Paulo, 1938. Graduated from the School of Architecture and Urbanism, University of São Paulo, 1960

ルイ・オータケ
1938年サンパウロに生まれる。1960年サンパウロ大学建築・都市計画科卒業。
事務所の設立は1962年。

AGUAS DE PRATA BALNEARY
Location: Aguas da Prata, São Paulo, 1974
Collaborator: Masayoshi Kamimura
Consultant: Siguer Mitsutani (Structural)
Igor Sresnewsky (Acoustic)
Escr. Tec. Enio José Ribeiro (Hydraulic)
Escr. Tec. Jose Roberto Ferreira (Electrical)
Odilea Helena Setti Toscano (Landscape)
Photographers: Cristiano Mascaro, Lucio Gomes Machado
Constructor: Clywaldo Pessanha Henriques Ltda

*

ARARAQUARA UNIVERSITY CAMPUS
Location: Araraquara, São Paulo, 1974
Collaborator: Massayoshi Kamimura
Consultant: Siguer Mitsutani (Structural), Escr. Tec. Enio Jose Riberio (Hydraulic), Escr. Tec. Jose Roberto Ferreira (Electrical), Odilea Helena Setti Toscano (Landscape)
Photographers: Cristiano Mascaro, Lucio Gomes Machado
Constructor: COCIBRA, Construtora Privato & Cia

Architects

Joao Walter Toscano Arquitetos Associados LTDA
Established in 1957.
João Walter Toscano
Born in Itu, São Paulo, 1933. Graduated from the School of Architecture and Urbanism, University of São Paulo, 1956.
Odilea Helena Setti Toscano
Born in São Bernardo do Campo, São Paulo, 1934. Graduated from the School of Architecture and Urbanism, University of São Paulo, 1956.

ジョアオ・W・トスカーノ
1933年サンパウロに生まれる。1956年サンパウロ大学建築・都市計画科卒業。
オディレア・H・S・トスカーノ
1934年サンパウロに生まれる。1956年サンパウロ大学建築・都市計画科卒業。
事務所の設立は1957年。

JULIO DE MESQUITA FILHO HOSPITAL
Location: Marginal do Tietê, São Paulo

Architects

Fabio Penteado, Teru Tamaki e Arquitetos Associados S/C LTDA
Established in 1968.
Fabio Moura Penteado
Born in São Paulo, 1929. Graduated from the School of Architecture, Mackenzie University, 1953.
Teru Tamaki
Graduated from School of Architecture and Urbanism, University of São Paulo, 1962.

ファビオ・M・ペンテアド
1929年サンパウロに生まれる。1953年マッケンジー大学建築科卒業。
テル・タマキ
1962年サンパウロ大学建築・都市計画科卒業。
事務所の設立は1968年。

CALUX KINDERGARTEN
Location: São Bernardo do Campo, São Paulo, 1978

Architect

Paulo Mendes da Rocha
Born in Vitória, Espírito Santo, 1928. Graduated from the School of Architecture, Mackenzie University, 1954.

パウロ・M・ダ・ローシャ
1928年エスピリト・サントに生まれる。1954年マッケンジー大学卒業。

160

CECAP TAUBATÉ HOUSING DEVELOPMENT
Location: Quiririm, Taubaté, São Paulo, 1973
Consultant: Minor Nagao (Structural), STECIL (Mechanical), Ayako Nishikawa (Landscape)

*

MORUMBY OFFICE BUILDING
Location: R. George Eastman, Morumbi, São Paulo, 1972
Consultant: J. K. & J. Z KURKDJAN (Structural), THERMOPLAN (Air conditioning), CGB INSTALAÇÕES (Mechanical), MAG ENGENHEIROS ASSOCIADOS (Foundation)

*

J. O. MAIA RESIDENCE
Location: R. Albert Einstein, Morumbi, São Paulo, 1973
Consultant: J.K. & J. Z. KURKDJAN (Structural), PHE PROJETOS (Mechanical), Ayako Nishikawa (Landscape)

*

VERONEZZI RESIDENCE
Location: R. Heron Domingues, São Paulo, 1977
Consultant: J. K. & J. Z. KURKDJAN (Structural), THERMOPLAN (Air conditioning), PHE PROJETOS (Mechanical), MAG ENGENHEIROS ASSOCIADOS (Foundation)

Architects

Bonilha & Sancovski Arquitetos SC LTDA
Established in 1962.
Jeronimo Bonilha Esteves
Born in Garça, 1933. Graduated from the School of Architecture and Urbanism, University of São Paulo, 1957.
Israel Sancovski
Born in São Paulo, 1935. Graduated from the School of Architecture and Urbanism, University of São Paulo, 1957.

J・ボニーリャ・エステヴェス
1933年ガルシャに生まれる。1957年サンパウロ大学建築・都市計画科卒業。
イスラエル・サンコーヴィスキー
1935年サンパウロに生まれる。1957年サンパウロ大学建築・都市計画科卒業。
事務所の設立は1962年。

PIRAQUÊ INDUSTRY
Location: Madureira, Rio de Janeiro, 1977
Consultant: PROMON ENGENHARIA (Engineering), José Roberto Parisi Eng. (Structural)
Photographer: José Moscardi

*

PONTE PEQUENA METRO STATION
Location: Ponte Pequena, São Paulo, 1973
Collaborator: Joao Batista Correa, Setsuo Hori
Consultant: ETEP ENGENHARIA
Photographer: José Moscardi

Architect

Marcello Accioly Fragelli
Born in Rio de Janeiro, 1928. Graduated from the School of Architecture, University of Brazil, 1952.

マルセーロ・A・フランジェリ
1928年リオデジャネイロに生まれる。1952年ブラジル大学建築科卒業。

L. GUEDES RESIDENCE
Location: São Paulo, 1971

*

MOREAU RESIDENCE
Location: Ibiúna, São Paulo, 1978

*

BEER RESIDENCE
Location: R. Jacupiranga, São Paulo, 1976
Photographer: José Moscardi

*

CARAIBA NEW TOWN
Location: Caraiba, Bahia

Architect

Arquiteto Joaquim Guedes e Associados
Established in 1955.
Joaquim Guedes
Born in São Paulo, 1932. Graduated from the School of Architecture and Urbanism, University of São Paulo, 1954.

ジョアキン・ゲーデス
1932年サンパウロに生まれる。1954年サンパウロ大学建築・都市計画科卒業。
事務所の設立は1955年。

IBM EDUCATIONAL CENTRE
Location: Gávea, Rio de Janeiro
Architect: Davino Pontual, Paulo S. Pires, Sergio Porto
Consultant: Escritorio de Engenharia Antonio Alves de Noronha, Eng. Ronaldo Uchoa (Structural), Alamo Engenharia, Eng. Osvaldo Gil Matias (Electrical and Plumbing), Moraes e Vaisberg Cia., Eng. G. Vaisberg and Nildo de Jesus Domingues (Air Conditioning), Flavio Brito Pereira (Landscape), Carlos Eugenio Hime (Acoustic)
Constructor: HB Engenharia
Collaborator: João Nascimento Ribeiro, Ana Maria Pires Ribeiro

Architects

Pontual Associados; Arquitetura e Planejamento; LTDA
Established in 1960.
Davino Pontual
Born in Recife, 1938. Graduated from the National School of Architecture, University of Brazil, 1963
Paulo de Souza Pires
Born in Rio de Janeiro, December 1938. Graduated from the National Technical School, 1958
Sergio Porto
Born in Rio de Janeiro, 1934. Graduated from the National School of Architecture, University of Brazil, 1957
Artur Licio Marques Pontual (died 1972)
Flavio O. Ferreira (withdrew in 1979)

ダヴィノ・ポントゥアール
1938年レシフェに生まれる。1963年ブラジル大学建築科卒業。

パウロ・デ・S・ピレス
1938年リオデジャネイロに生まれる。1958年国立工科学校卒業。

セルジオ・ポルト
1934年リオデジャネイロに生まれる。1957年ブラジル大学建築科卒業。

アルトゥール・L・M・ポントゥアール（1972年没）
フラヴィオ・O・フェレイラ（1979年退所）
事務所の設立は1960年。

COSAMA RESERVOIR
Location: Manaus, Amazonas, 1972
Constructor: CONSTRUTORA NORBERTO ODERBRECHT

*

SHUSTER RESIDENCE
Location: Tarumã, Amazonas

*

PORTO RESIDENCE
Location: Manaus, Amazonas, 1971

Architects

Severiano Mario Porto, Arquitetura e Planejamento LTDA
Established in 1954.
Severiano Mario Porto
Born in Rio de Janeiro, 1930. Graduated from the National School of Architecture, University of Brazil, 1954.
Mario Emilio Ribeiro, Architect
Arnoldo Gomes da Costa, Engineer
Álvaro Regis de Menezes, Economist

S・マリオ・ポルト
1930年リオデジャネイロに生まれる。1954年ブラジル大学建築科卒業。
マリオ・E・リベイロ：建築家
アーノルド・G・ダ・コスタ：エンジニア
アルヴァ・R・デ・メネセス：エコノミスト
事務所の設立は1954年。

ZANETTINI RESIDENCE
Location: Pereiras, Atibaia, São Paulo, 1975

*

BANESPA TUTOIA BANK
Location: Paraiso, São Paulo, 1978

Architect

Arquiteto Siegbert Zanettini
Established in 1960.
Siegbert Zanettini
Born in 1934. Graduated from the School of Architecture and Urbanism, University of São Paulo, 1959.

シーギベルチ・ザネチーニ
1934年に生まれる。1959年サンパウロ大学建築・都市計画科卒業。
事務所の設立は1960年。

HOSPITAL FOR THE HANDICAPPED
Location: Brasília, DF, 1976
Assistant: Ciaudio Bois Duarte, José Lourenço de Souza, Kristian Schiel, Marco Antônio Pinheiro, Oscar Borges Kneipp, Rubens D. Lara Arruda, Walter K. Hanashiro
Consultant: PROJECTUM ENGENHARIA (Structural), ACQUALUX (Mechanical)
Invited Artist: Athos Bulcão
Constructor: Joaquim Ferreira Cambraia Eng., SIT Sociedade de instalações Técnicas S.A.

*

ADMINISTRATIVE CENTER OF BAHIA
Location: Salvador, Bahia
Assistant: Fernando J. Ferreira de Andrade, José Paulo de Bens, Maria F. Tereza Lafetá, Oscar Borges Kneipp, Oswaldo Cintra de Carvalho
Consultant: WALTER & WALTER, PROJECTUM ENGENHARIA (Structural), ACQUALUX (Mechanical), Conrado Silva de Marco (Acoustic), Alda Rabello Cunha (Landscape)
Invited Artist: Athos Bulcão
Constructor: CONCIC Portuária
Photographers: Luiz Carlos Homana, A. Grebler

*

CAB CHAPEL
Location: Salvador, Bahia, 1974
Assistant: Dimitri Tavares Vila Nova, José Luiz Menezes, Kristian Schiel, Rubens D. Lara Arruda
Consultant: WALTER & WALTER (Structural), ACQUALUX (Mechanical), Conrado Silva de Marco (Acoustic), Alda Rabello Cunha (Landscape)
Photographers: Luiz Carlos Homam, GRUPO ZAZ

Architect

João Filgueiras Lima
Born in Rio de Janeiro, 1932. Graduated from the National School of Architecture, University of Brazil, 1955.

ジョアオ・F・リーマ
1932年リオデジャネイロに生まれる。1955年ブラジル大学建築科卒業。

MIGUEL DE CERVANTES HIGH SCHOOL
Location: Morumbi, São Paulo, 1978
Principal Architect: Antonio Carlos Sant'Anna Jr.
Consultant: Carlos Eduardo de Paula Pessoa (Structural), Helio Santiago (Electrical), Airton S.L.Viana (Hydraulic), Igor Sresnewsky (Acoustic), Fernando Chacel (Landscape)

Architects

Rino Levi Arquitetos Associados LTDA
Established in 1927.
Roberto Cerqueira Cesar
Born in São Paulo, 1917. Graduated from the Course of Architecture, Politechnic School of São Paulo.
Luiz Roberto Carvalho Franco
Born in Araras, São Paulo, 1926. Graduated from the School of Architecture and Urbanism, Mackenzie University.
Paulo Julio Valentino Bruna
Born in São Paulo, 1941. Graduated from the School of Architecture and Urbanism, University of São Paulo.

ロベルト・C・セザール
1917年サンパウロに生まれる。サンパウロ工業学校建築科卒業。
ルイス・R・カルバロ・フランコ
1926年サンパウロに生まれる。マッケンジー大学建築科卒業。
パウロ・J・V・ブルナ
1941年サンパウロを生まれる。サンパウロ大学建築・都市計画科卒業。
事務所の設立は1929年。

CAETANO DE CAMPOS TRANING SCHOOL
Location: Aclimação, São Paulo, 1976

*

CEESP TIRADENTES BANK
Location: Av. Tiradentes, São Paulo, 1977

*

IGUATEMI BUILDING
Location: Av. Faria Lima, São Paulo, 1973

*

CAMPOS DO JORDÃO HALL
Location: Campos do Jordão, São Paulo, 1978

Architects

161

Croce, Aflalo & Gasperini Arquitetos LTDA
Established in 1962.
Plinio Croce
Born in São Paulo, 1921. Graduated from the School of Engineering and Architecture, Mackenzie University, São Paulo, 1946.
Roberto Aflalo
Born in São Paulo, 1926. Graduated from the School of Architecture and Urbanism, Mackenzie University, São Paulo, 1950.
Gian Carlo Gasperini
Born in Italy, 1926. Graduated from University of Brazil, Rio de Janeiro, 1949.

プリニオ・クロッチェ
1921年サンパウロに生まれる.1946年マッケンジー大学建築工学科卒業.

ロベルト・アフラーロ
1926年サンパウロに生まれる.1950年マッケンジー大学建築・都市計画科卒業.

ジャン・C・ガスペリーニ
1926年イタリアに生まれる.1949年ブラジル大学卒業.
事務所の設立は1962年.

SIGRIST RESIDENCE
Location: Morumbi, São Paulo, 1976
Consultant: MAUBERTEC (Structural), SPIG (Mechanical)

*

ALMEIDA RESIDENCE
Location: São Paulo, 1977
Consultant: Faustino M. da Silva (Structural), Carlos Ripper (Mechanical), J. Miret Serra (Electrical)

*

DEFINE RESIDENCE
Location: São Paulo, 1978
Consultant: Faustino Maximo da Silva (Structural), Eurico Marques (Mechan./Electrical)

Architect

Eduardo de Almeida
Born in 1933. Graduated from the School of Architecture and Urbanism, University of São Paulo, 1960.

エドゥアルド・デ・アウメイダ
1933年に生まれる.1960年サンパウロ大学建築・都市計画科卒業.

ANNEX FOR THE LEGISLATIVE ASSEMBLY
Location: Curitiba, Paraná

*

PERNAMBUCO EXPO CENTRE
Location: Recife, Pernambuco

*

TERRAFOTO HEADQUARTER
Location: Embu, São Paulo

Architects

Ramalho & Oba Arquitetos
Joel Ramalho Junior
Born in Tombos, Minas Gerais, 1934. Graduated from the School of Architecture, Mackenzie University, 1959.
Leonardo Toshiaki Oba
Born in Londrina, Paraná, 1950. Graduated from the School of Architecture and Urbanism, Federal University of Paraná, 1972.
Guilherme Zamoner Neto
Born in Londrina, Paraná, 1950. Graduated from the School of Architecture and Urbanism, Federal University of Paraná, 1974.

ジョエル・ラマーリョ Jr.
1934年に生まれる.1959年マッケンジー大学建築科卒業.

レオナルド・T・オーバ
1950年パラナ州に生まれる.1972年パラナ大学建築・都市計画科卒業.

G・ザモネール・ネット
1950年パラナ州に生まれる.1974年パラナ大学建築・都市計画科卒業.

ACARPA HEADQUARTER
Location: R. das Bandeiras, Curitiba, Paraná
Architects: Luiz Forte Netto, Orlando Busarello, Dilva C.S. Busarello, Adolfo Sakaguti

Architects

Luiz Forte Netto
Born in São paulo, 1935. Graduated from the School of Architecture and Urbanism, Mackenzie University, 1958.
Orlando Busarello
Born in Taió, Santa Catarina, 1946. Graduated from the School of Architecture and Urbanism, Federal University of Paraná.
Dilva Candida Slomp Busarello
Born in Caçador, Santa Catarina, 1947. Graduated from the School of Architecture and Urbanism, Federal University of Paraná, 1970.
Adolfo Sakaguti
Born in Paraná, 1954. Graduated from the School of Architecture and Urbanism, Federal University of Paraná, 1976.
Vicente Ferreira de Castro Neto
Born in Rio de Janeiro, 1943. Graduated from the School of Engineering, Federal University of Paraná, 1966.

ルイス・フォルテ・ネット
1935年サンパウロに生まれる.1958年マッケンジー大学建築・都市計画科卒業.

オーランド・ブサレーロ
1946年サンタ・カタリナ州に生まれる.パラナ大学建築・都市計画科卒業.

ディルバ・C・S・ブサレーロ
1947年サンタ・カタリナ州に生まれる.1970年パラナ大学建築・都市計画科卒業.

アドルフォ・サカグチ
1954年パラナに生まれる.1976年パラナ大学建築・都市計画科卒業.

ビセンテ・F・C・ネット
1943年リオデジャネイロに生まれる.1966年パラナ大学卒業.

ERPLAN HEADQUATERS
Location: Ribeirão Prêto, São Paulo

Architects

Tamar Ferreira De Lima
Born in Recife, Pernambuco, 1945. Graduated from the School of Architecture, Pernambuco University, 1970.
Augusto Cesar Laranjeira Machado
Born in Recife, Pernambuco, 1946. Graduated from the School of Architecture, Pernambuco University, 1970.
Carlos Hideki Matsuzawa
Born in Lins, São Paulo, 1952. Graduated from the School of Architecture and Urbanism, University of São Paulo, 1976.
Humberto Tetsuya Yamaki
Born in São Paulo, 1952. Graduated from the School of Architecture and Urbanism, University of Sao Paulo, 1976.

タマール・F・デ・リーマ
1945年ペルナンブーコに生まれる.1970年ペルナンブーコ大学建築科卒業.

アウグスト・C・L・マシャード
1946年ペルナンブーコに生まれる.1970年ペルナンブーコ大学建築科卒業.

カルロス・ヒデキ・マツザワ
1952年サンパウロに生まれる.1976年サンパウロ大学建築・都市計画科卒業.

ウンベルト・T・ヤマキ
1952年サンパウロに生まれる.1976年サンパウロ大学建築・都市計画科卒業.

情報の洪水といわれる今日の状況の中で，ともすれば私たちは，表面のみに目を奪われ，真に必要なもの，最も大切なことを見失いかねません．

PROCESS：ARCHITECTUREは，常に私たちに欠くことのできない重要なテーマの厳選に努めています．

PROCESS：ARCHITECTUREは，

●雑誌と書籍の両方の長所を備えた新しいタイプの出版物です．

●各号ごとにそれぞれ一つのテーマをとりあげます．

●各テーマにふさわしい専門家を，責任編集者としています．

●視覚を重視し，写真・図版・スケッチなどは，他に類をみないほど豊富に収載します．

●専門書というにたる十分な内容を備え，参考資料としても高い評価を得ています．

●総合芸術であり，総合技術である ARCHITECTURE ととり組むにあたり，テーマは広くインテリア・デザインから環境問題にまで及びますが，その主体は常に人間です．

●最新建築のデザインを単にファッションとして扱うことに終始する態度はとりません．

●私たちの目，耳，足で確め，十分に消化したものを，活きた情報として提供します．

●無批判に情報を流すのではなく，出版に値すると判断された情報のみを，思想，信条，派閥，かたよった考え方などにとらわれることなく，とりあげます．

PROCESS：ARCHITECTUREは，このような方針のもとに努力を重ねてまいりますが，最終的な判断，評価を下すのは読者の皆さんです．これからも皆さんのご理解とご支援を期待してやみません．

発行人　室谷　文治

●PROCESS：ARCHITECTURE is a new type of publication combining the best of both book and magazine forms.

●Each issue treats one theme only.

●Each issue is managed by an editor-in-charge who is a professional in the field which the issue treats.

●Visual representation is emphasized with an abundance of photographs, drawings, and sketches.

●As a professional publication, the contents are of such value that every issue may be saved for reference.

●As architecture is an integrated art and an integrated technology, the themes range from interior design to environmental concerns, always stressing human values.

●PROCESS：ARCHITECTURE goes beyond the ''latest'' and fads in architecture.

●All our information must be fresh；we publish only what we ourselves have ascertained and digested.

●It is our policy to remain free of predetermined concepts and cliques.

We offer our readers the information that will be of most value to them.

●No. I ●現代北欧建築——A Perspective of Modern Scandinavian Architecture————品切れ　Sold out

●No. 2 ●ミッチェル／ジョゴラ・アーキテクツ——Mitchell／Giurgola Architects————品切れ　Sold out

●No. 3 ●住民参加のコミュニティ・デザイン——Community Design：By the People————¥2700

●No. 4 ●ローレンス・ハルプリン——Lawrence Halprin————品切れ　Sold out

●No. 5 ●現代カナダ建築——A Perspective of Modern Canadian Architecture————¥2900

●No. 6 ●ソーラー・アーキテクチュア——Solar Architecture————品切れ　Sold out

●No. 7 ●現代アメリカ住宅——Modern Houses in America————品切れ　Sold out

●No. 8 ●ウルリック・フランツェン——Ulrich Franzen————¥2700

●No. 9 ●世界の新しい都市交通——New Transport Systems in the World————¥2900

●No.10●ヒュー・スタビンズ——Hugh Stubbins————¥2900

●No.11●ハリー・ウィーズ——Harry Weese————¥2900

●No.12●現代アメリカ低層ハウジング：郊外篇——Low-Rise Housing in America：The Suburban Scene——¥2900

●No.13●アメリカのインテリア・デザイン——Interior Design Planned Space————¥2900

●No.14●現代アメリカ低層ハウジング：都市編——Low-Rise Housing in America：The Urban Scene——¥2900

●No.15●風土と建築：西南アジアの集落と住居——Indigenous Settlements in Southwest Asia————¥2900

●No.16●南欧の広場——Plazas of Southern Europe————¥3300

・いずれも在庫僅少です．お早めに最寄りの書店にお申し込み下さい．

・予約購読をお受けいたしております．くわしくは当社営業部にお問い合わせ下さい．

・No. Iより No.10までを一組としてセット販売いたしております．在庫僅少，定価27000円　（国内送料当社負担）．

●株式会社 プロセス アーキテクチュア

東京都文京区小石川3-1-3

電話03-816-1695・1696

● Next Issue of Process : Architecture (Advertisement)

MODERN WOODEN HOUSES
現代木造住宅

● 8月15日発売予定 ● 予価2900円

人間の生活の基本の場は住宅にあり，建築の原点もまた住宅にある．建築とは何か，生活の場とは何かを問う時，そこに住宅をはずすことは出来ない．それゆえに，複雑な現代生活の中での住宅の意味を問いつめることは，建築家のみならず一般の人々にとっても重要なことである．

本特集は上述の点を踏まえながら，種々様々の材料で建設されているアメリカの現代住宅の中から，主体構造に「木」を用いた，いわゆる「木造住宅」に焦点を当て，現代住宅の形態・空間構成・デザイン傾向について，多くの例題を通して考察したものである．

● 論文：アメリカの木造住宅――スタンリー・アバークロンビー
● 作品：33題
● 設計者：マイロン・ゴールドフィンガー／グラハム・ガンド・アソシエイツ／スタンリー・タイガーマン／ウェンデル・H・ラヴェット／ヒュー・ニューウェル・ジェイコブスン／ブース・ネイグル・アンド・ハートレイ／アルフレッド・デ・ヴィド／グワスメイ・シーゲル・アーキテクツ／マルセル・ブロイヤー・アソシエイツ／ビッセル・アンド・ウェルズ／他．

This issue presents single-family houses in America by focussing on wood frame as a main structural system. Thirty-three works (built from 1975 up to the present) selected from all parts of the United States for this issue are typical design examples available today to show the recent trends of designing form and space in wooden house. Each work is presented with a description by architect along with many photographs and drawings.

● Article :
AMERICAN WOOD HOUSES
by Stanley Abercrombie

● Architects :
Myron Goldfinger／Graham Gund Associates／Stanley Tigerman／Wendell H. Lovett／Hugh Newell Jacobsen／Booth Nagle & Hartray／Alfredo De Vido／Gwathmey Siegel Architects／Marcel Breuer Associates／Bissell & Wells／Others.

PRIVATE HOUSE in Long Island, Architect : Myron Goldfinger, Photo : Norman McGrath